"A timely concept, powerfı
and formulated through ex
experience and research."

DAITHÍ MAC SÍTHIGH, HEAD OF
IADT DÚN LAOGHAIRE

INCLUSIVE INTELLIGENCE

How to be a Role Model for Diversity and Inclusion in the Workplace

FURKAN KARAYEL

MULTI-AWARD-WINNING GLOBAL DIVERSITY AND INCLUSION LEADER

Inclusive Intelligence

First published in 2021 by

Panoma Press Ltd
48 St Vincent Drive, St Albans, Herts, AL1 5SJ, UK
info@panomapress.com
www.panomapress.com

Book layout by Neil Coe.

978-1-784529-60-4

A CIP catalogue record for this book is available from the British Library.

This book is available online and in bookstores.

This book is dedicated to my large family, the Karayel family of Giresun, Turkey. Especially to my mother Benan Karayel and my father Ahmet Karayel, who built a safe, compassionate and nurturing family for me and my siblings to grow up in, who believed in me from my childhood days and have passionately supported me in all my decisions throughout my life.

To my siblings Elif, Zeynep, Ayşegül, Fatih and Bedir for bringing joy to my life every day.

To the people of Ireland for embracing me and my authentic self, opening their beautiful doors and warm hearts with 'céad míle fáilte' and making Ireland the place I call 'home'.

Testimonials

"A timely concept, powerfully argued, and formulated through extensive experience and research."

Daithí Mac Síthigh, head of research, Institute of Art, Design + Technology (IADT)

"The pandemic has been challenging and has given us few benefits, but one fantastic plus is that the pandemic gave Furkan Karayel time to write this amazing book. In it, she tackles the subject of diversity and inclusion with eye-opening clarity. She helps us to define terms that can sometimes feel as hazy as clouds. And her writing style is easy to read and heightens our understanding of a topic that often feels uncomfortable, complicated, and unclear.

"With openness and honesty, Furkan takes us on a journey of her truth and shares her struggles. Along the way, she helps us define our authentic selves. You can tell that she genuinely cares and wants to help companies and individuals progress in diversity and inclusion.

"While this book will help you elevate your organisation's attention to diversity and inclusion, the book also gives you a clear path of self-improvement with exercises like journaling, surveys, and interviewing. I think everyone from the CEO to the entry-level staff will benefit from reading this book."

Kimberly Mosley, CAE, executive director, Digital Analytics Association

"An essential book that all leaders must read to nurture self-awareness, foster authenticity, develop cultural wisdom and enhance personal accountability. A practical self-help guide with a plethora of useful examples, activities and exercises for clarity – every inclusive leader can vastly benefit from reading this whether they are new to the conversation or have long been part of it."

Hira Ali, author of *Her Way to The Top: A Guide to Smashing the Glass Ceiling* and *Her Allies: A Practical Toolkit to Help Men Lead Through Advocacy*

"Based on lived experience, backed by science, this book is generous, practical, and packed with reflections, tips, tools, activities and easily applied interventions. The author demystifies diversity, equality and inclusion concepts by breaking them down to actionable steps that nudge the reader towards active allyship. Making inclusion accessible, this book walks you through Inclusive Leadership and to Positive Change – for individuals, teams and organisations alike. This book walks its talk and is a must-have on every leader's bookshelf."

Jen Martin, psychological coach

"Let me share the secret resource that is Furkan Karayel with you. Her passion and sincerity shine throughout her new *Inclusive Intelligence* book and the personal stories she shares make key concepts crystal clear. The activities, resources and tools provided build an increased awareness cemented by reflections to match these approaches to your own situation. Invest some time to become a more effective leader and team member!"

Roxanne Gimbel, systems delivery consultant

"Must say Furkan Karayel is one of the most interesting and inspirational people I have met in a long while. A fantastic ambassador and advocate for diversity and inclusion in Ireland and beyond. If you have not yet met Furkan then you should rectify that soonest! Insightful and articulate on a range of topics from diversity and inclusion, education, startup culture and technology to public speaking."

Adrian Whelan, senior vice president, Brown Brothers Harriman

"Furkan Karayel showcases her wealth of knowledge, depth of experience, and authenticity in *Inclusive Intelligence: How to Be a Role Model for Diversity and Inclusion in the Workplace*. The book provides business leaders with strong and clear takeaways that they can implement in their own organisations right away. Hope there are more books like this to follow."

David Watters, founder, Ignite X and Dive in With Watters

"I first met Furkan when Lean-In-Ireland had invited her to form part of a panel discussion at the House of Lords. Furkan and I went on to record an episode of the *Legends & Legacy* YouTube show together since.

"Furkan is a lady I admire, who I have watched bring people together, standing up for inequality and inclusivity. Furkan quickly captures the hearts of people and in her heart lies a drive for fairness. This lady is a talented, quietly driven, focused professional on a mission to speak her truth, teaching others as she goes."

Breda McCague, co-founder of Lean-In-Ireland, motivational speaker, mind mastery coach

Acknowledgements

I would like to thank everyone who helped me on this journey of writing this book for their endless support including Deborah Somorin, Aldagh McDonogh, Roxanne Gimbel, Adrian Whelan, Jen Martin, Maura McAdam, Sarah Cunningham, Ruth Leonard, Breda McCague, Grace Yan, David Watters, Daithí Mac Síthigh, Hira Ali, Kimberly Mosley, Máirín Murray, Therese Moylan, Miren-Maialen Samper, Susan Moran, Magdalena Kuraczowska, Joanne Kenney, Gina Oglesby, Helen Zidon, Adaku Ezeudo, Dawn Leane, Silvija Delekovcan, Mary Anne O'Carroll, Asif Sadiq, Louise Tierney, Francy Sanchez, Lisa McKenna, Judith Spring leadership class, Roisin Lyons, Dublin City University Practicum students including, Killian Davis, Preciosa Vaz, Madhura Chatterjee, Isha Rai, Vagish Bhardwaj, Dún Laoghaire Institute Of Art Design + Technology and Huckletree.

Also, I would like to thank everyone who inspires me, including Amy Cuddy, Brené Brown, Bill George, Arianna Huffington, Daniel Goleman, Adam Grant, Dr Ebun Joseph, Malala Yousafzai, Oprah Winfrey, Susan Cain, Francesca Gino and Gabor Maté.

Author's Note

"Anonymous was a woman."

Virginia Woolf

I held myself back from speaking for so many years owing to my introverted personality, imposter syndrome, my self-criticism, my perfectionism and being afraid to be judged by others. In fact, I have always been the quietest child in my family of six, and mostly kept my ideas anonymously in my blogs or journals.

However, the one thing missing from all those blogs and articles was ME. Over the years, I built up so many untold stories inside me that I could no longer hold them in.

Day by day, the more I shared my ideas with people, especially people from many different backgrounds, the more I found similarities between us. As a result, I started sharing more, especially with my authentic self.

Why does this book matter?

My aim in writing this book is to bring another perspective to your leadership style and help you to build happier workplaces where everyone thrives with their authentic selves.

Inclusive Intelligence is the meeting point of Emotional Intelligence and inclusive leadership. Its methodology is based on a series of interviews and years of detailed research conducted with team leaders and managers in a variety of global companies. We found a pattern in some leaders who naturally excelled at inclusive leadership even though they were unaware of it and unable to define it.

This book describes the skills these leaders have in common and how they made inclusion part of their daily agenda and became role models through their incredible work.

My aim throughout the book has been to keep my language clear and simple, my examples real and relevant, and my recommendations practical and inspiring for you.

You must be wondering at this stage what led me to build a career like this. Here is my answer.

I started my career as a software engineer in a multinational tech company in Ireland. You might already be familiar with the lack of female representation in the technology industry.

I was working in my dream job as a software engineer; however, I was mostly the only representative of my identity as a Turk, my gender as a woman, my religion as a Muslim and my personality as an introvert within the teams I worked in.

Later in my career I also saw that women were always a minority in the leadership positions of technology companies. Women from different ethnic backgrounds in leadership roles did not even exist. This was my first wake up call.

After diversity and inclusion became a trend for technology companies, I again observed that diversity and inclusion-related decisions were being taken by top managers who had no experience of being part of a minority. While diversity and inclusion activities turned out to be one of the best PR tools for media purposes, action was always missing. Additionally, I had a manager who did not know how to deal with me.

All of this led me to set up Diversein. As a company, we help multinational companies to develop diversity inclusion programmes to further their journey into an authentic inclusion.

As an inclusive leadership advisor, I train leaders to practise Inclusive Intelligence pillars on a daily basis and eventually become role models in the workplace.

I hope my story resonates with you and your journey at some point.

I would like to thank you for giving up your precious time to read this book and for your willingness to enhance your Inclusive Intelligence.

Remember, Inclusive Intelligence is a journey. The earlier you start on the journey, the further you go.

Now, it's time to get your favourite drink, a journal and a pen. Let's get started.

Furkan Karayel

Timeline of the book

12th January 2020. I was sitting in the middle seat on a packed flight from Dublin to London Heathrow. I started getting a bit nervous because we were already 30 minutes late taking off. If we had left on time, we would already be getting ready to land by this time – Dublin to London only takes about 45 minutes. I had only allowed one and a half hours to catch my connecting flight to Dallas, Texas.

With anxiety on my face, I asked the British Airways hostess if I would be able to catch my next flight on time. She nodded at me with a big smile and reassuring look on her face. I chose to trust her and decided to focus on something else. So, I took my notebook out of my bag and started writing the first words of the book you are currently holding in your hands. By the time we took off, I had already written six full pages.

25th January 2020. Plano, Texas. My flight back to Dublin was the next day and I had just had the two most productive weeks of my life. With the help of jet lag, I had been waking up around 4.30am without an alarm, then settling down at my desk and writing, writing and writing until breakfast, which started at around 8.30am. I would be back in my room by 9.00am and phoned my parents in Turkey (the best time to call them due to the 8 hours' time difference). On the news, I occasionally saw that there was a new virus spreading around the world – almost 70 cases had been discovered in China and one case in Texas.

24th March 2020. Dublin was officially under lockdown. I had already finished proofreading my book and was planning to record its online course videos in late March. With the lockdown, everything stopped and I took a long break until the end of Ramadan (end of May).

8th September 2020. We launched the online course with a webinar. I was very excited as I spent most of the summer working on it, editing chapters and getting initial feedback from a few people. It all looked very promising.

7th June 2021. More than a year on, all my attempts at finding a publisher had failed big time.

21st June 2021. I met Mindy from Panoma Press and the rest is history.

Contents

DIVERSITY IS YOU. BECAUSE YOU ARE UNIQUE. INCLUSION IS ACCEPTING YOU. BECAUSE YOU MATTER.

Introduction: What is Inclusive Intelligence?

Organisations look very different today from what they did 50 or 60 years ago. Physically and psychologically. Today, we do not just look for jobs that pay well. We also look for jobs that make us feel good, no matter who we are and where we are.

More and more companies embrace diversity, promoting awareness of diversity and inclusion and expanding the time and budget they spend on it. Studies show that diversity and inclusion in the workplace improve our relationships as a team, make us feel better and improve our wellbeing as well as product quality, team performance and business revenue (Menzies 2018; Dixon-Fyle et al. 2020; Gaudiano 2020).

This is especially true in multinational companies where many employees of different cultural backgrounds work under the same roof for many years.

Previous Teams	Today's Teams
Homogeneous	Diverse
Slow paced	Fast paced
Inflexible	Flexible
Hierarchical	Horizontal

What do I mean by diversity and inclusion?

Here is my definition:

> Diversity is you. Because you are unique. Inclusion is accepting you. Because you matter.
>
> Diversity is being invited to the table. Inclusion is sharing the cake fairly.

In a workplace, diversity means building balanced harmony with a range of gender, ethnicity, culture, age, experience, preference, abilities, status, religion, socio-economic backgrounds and thoughts. Inclusion is accepting everyone as a unique and valued element of this harmony.

If you are committed to being a role model in this area, then I challenge you to come up with your own definition of diversity and inclusion and start using it in your conversations.

With the prioritisation of diversity increasing rapidly, the importance of inclusive leadership is coming into focus. The article 'Unraveling the Diversity-Performance Link in Multicultural Teams' by Stahl, Maznevski, Voigt, Jonsen shows that (Jonsen et al. 2007):

- Compared to homogenous teams, diverse teams take longer to stabilise their performance.
- Without inclusive leadership, diverse teams cannot perform and unlock the potential that diversity provides.
- Without inclusive leadership, diversity recruitment and initiatives are not sustainable and often result in failure.

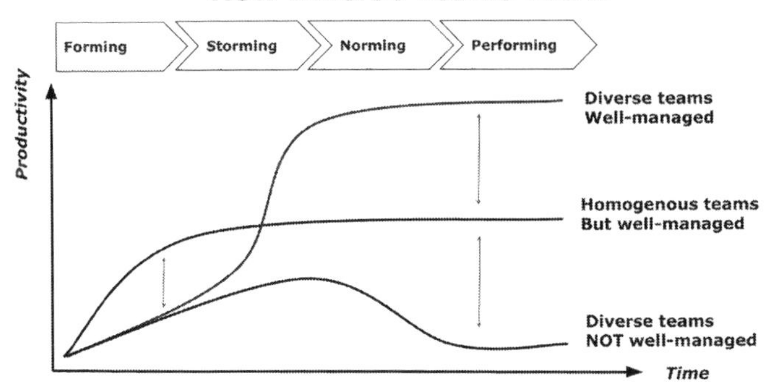

Source: *"Unraveling the Diversity-Performance Link in Multicultural Teams", by Stahl, Maznevski, Voigt and Jonsen, 2007*

Exit surveys by LinkedIn show that dissatisfaction with senior management is the second biggest reason why people leave their jobs, with a rating as high as 41 per cent. The biggest reason, with a rating of 46 per cent, is the lack of opportunities for advancement, which could in some cases also be linked to dissatisfaction with senior management (Cruz et al. 2015).

If you look at average talent retention rates in multinational companies today, it is less than 2 years (Peterson 2017). According to a 2012 research study by the Center for American Progress, it costs up to $40k to replace a single talented individual (Boushey and Glynn 2012).

The employee retention rate of top tech companies according to Business Insider (August 2017) is as follows:

Facebook: 2.02 years

Google: 1.90 years

Oracle: 1.89 years

Apple: 1.85 years

Amazon: 1.84 years

Twitter: 1.83 years

Microsoft: 1.81 years

Airbnb: 1.64 years

Uber: 1.23 years

On the other hand, Deloitte's research shows that when managers embrace inclusive leadership practices, it has the greatest impact on organisations. Psychological safety, the sense of belonging, fairness, respect, inspiration and values increase by 70 per cent. In addition to this, team collaboration increases by 29 per cent. Decision making quality increases by 20 per cent. Team performance increases by 17 per cent (Bourke 2018).

Who would not want it?

What is Inclusive Intelligence?

Inclusive intelligence is internalising inclusion, opening up consciously to different views and perspectives and leading with authenticity. In other words, Inclusive Intelligence is understanding one's true self and one's core values, recognising and respecting other people's point of view, normalising inclusive behaviours on written and verbal interactions and on body language everyday so that these behaviours will become natural.

Inclusive Intelligence is the meeting point of Emotional Intelligence and inclusive leadership. Its methodology was developed based on a series of interviews and years of detailed research conducted with leaders of global companies. We found a pattern in some leaders who naturally excelled at inclusive leadership even though they were unaware of it.

This book describes the skills these leaders have in common, how they implement inclusion on a daily basis and how their incredible work makes them role models.

Our research shows that Inclusive Intelligence is best achieved by demonstrating these six skills in the workplace: self-awareness, empathy, engagement, cultural wisdom, accountability and commitment.

We refer to leaders who practise Inclusive Intelligence as inclusive leaders.

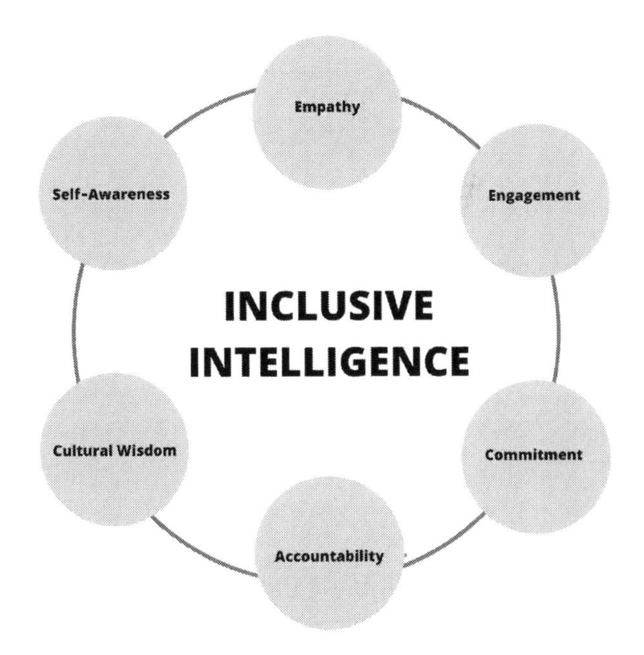

Working with a diverse range of managers from different part of the world, we often see that most managers feel positive about the concept but do not know how to implement inclusion in their daily tasks. In other words, they do not know what inclusion looks like. If you do not know what inclusion looks like, how can you know whether you are heading in the right direction and making any progress?

This book will guide you through the leadership skills and behaviours that can help you to be a consciously inclusive leader and will show you what an inclusively managed team looks like. If we do not know what inclusion looks like, we cannot tell if we are working in the right direction and making any progress.

Remember these skills are learnable. Nobody is born with them. All you need at the start is a 'genuine intention'. Being actively aware of these behaviours and injecting them into your day-to-day activities will have the best impact on your journey.

Here you are today reading this book. You already took the first step.

Now, let us take you forward!

Exercise: How do you define diversity and inclusion in your own words?

SELF-AWARENESS IS THE COURAGE
TO BE MORE COMFORTABLE WITH
YOURSELF AS A WHOLE.

CHAPTER ONE: SELF-AWARENESS

Introduction

What if you were able to discover something new about yourself that you have never known? In this first chapter, we will help you to discover your core 'you' by giving you key definitions, examples, practical actions and activities to build your self-awareness.

At the end of this chapter, you will be able to reflect and share what you did discover about yourself.

Let's get started.

"Yesterday I was clever, so I wanted to change the world. Today I am wise, so I am changing myself."

Rumi

Eoin was a senior marketing manager. By talking about the importance of diversity and inclusion within his organisation, he became the go-to person on that topic. Eoin had an extrovert personality and was usually the person leading the conversation in the room. At the end of meetings, he always asked if anyone had any questions and rarely encountered objections. Eoin rated himself as a highly inclusive leader. However, his colleagues did not agree, stating that Eoin did not give others equal opportunity to speak up at team meetings. Eoin was not aware of this at all.

Does this sound familiar to you? We have many colleagues at work who are not aware of their behaviour. If they were, they would happily change it in a heartbeat.

Self-awareness is the ability to consciously understand one's true self in terms of core values, motivators, strengths, weaknesses, needs, passions and lifetime experiences. When you are self-aware, you know your personal boundaries – what is acceptable to you and what is not. Are some of your boundaries flexible? What would be the cost of betraying them?

Self-awareness is finding the courage to ask difficult questions and be honest with yourself and others. Self-awareness is the courage to be more comfortable with yourself as a whole. It is the understanding of the reasons for your own behaviour. It is the ability to recognise yourself in others.

If you are self-aware, you are less surprised to hear what others think of you because you know how your actions are perceived by others. You are able to recognise your emotions and do not blame yourself for feeling them. The more self-aware you are, the more vulnerability you show by accepting the fact that you are a work in progress.

In a study, 69,000 managers assessed themselves and compared their self-perception with how other people perceived them. Surprisingly, the results showed that the most effective leaders were not those with the highest level of self-awareness (Zenger and Folkman 2019). Indeed, the more they underrated themselves, the more highly they were perceived as leaders.

In general, we are not good at estimating our own skills and abilities. The Johari Window places people into one of four categories: 'open' refers to being known to self and others; 'hidden' refers to being known to self but not to others; 'blind spot' refers to the things others know about us that we do not; 'unknown' refers to what is known neither to self nor to others (Wikimedia Foundation 2021).

	Known to Self	**Not known to Self**
Known to Others	**Open**	**Blind Spot**
Not known to Others	**Hidden**	**Unknown**

Johari Window (Luft, 1969)

What if highly effective managers could be highly self-aware too?

That last bit of research might make you wonder why managers and leaders need to be self-aware in the workplace. I hear you.

Let me explain with an example.

If you are working with a manager who has low self-awareness, she may not be managing the employee-manager relationship and you may often find yourself managing her instead. Although the employee-manager relationship works both ways, in this scenario the relationship is not comfortable.

It gets even more uncomfortable for employees who are in the indirect communication spectrum (people who don't directly say what they mean but choose an indirect meaning or word instead). It may get exhausting for you to have to explain yourself over and over.

Efficiency is only one side of the equation. Communication and relationships are everything for a manager. We like to work with managers we look up to and who inspire us. The chances are that a manager who is not very conscious of her behaviour and weaknesses would not inspire you greatly.

How can you be more self-aware?

Let's explore practical steps to build your self-awareness.

Action: Define your core values, motivators and passion

In other words, what makes you authentically 'you'? I have yet to see a great leader who is still trying to figure herself out.

Reflection: Consider what makes you authentically you.

Tips and tools: Be careful here not to describe what others expect you to be: it truly needs to be you. The Myers-Briggs Type Indicator ® test is a really good self-awareness tool that offers insight into how people perceive the world and make decisions. It looks at Introversion (I)/ Extraversion (E), Sensing (S)/Intuition (N), Thinking (T)/ Feeling (F) and Judging (J)/Perception (P). For example, I have an INFJ personality type. Knowing this helped me to become more conscious of my own communication style. Find out your personality type online – you can find the link in the references (Truity 2020).

Check out the list of values provided in the 'Core Values Activity'. It will make it easier for you to identify your core values.

Activity: core values

- Place a checkmark next to the 20 values that you feel are important to a life well lived. You may add your own core value words too.
- From the 20 values that you have checked, select 10 that you feel are critical to a life well lived and circle them.
- From the 10 values you circled, choose the five that are most important to you.

Core Values

Authenticity	Curiosity	Knowledge
Achievement	Determination	Leadership
Adventure	Fairness	Learning
Authority	Faith	Love
Autonomy	Fame	Loyalty
Balance	Friendships	Meaningful Work
Beauty	Fun	Openness
Boldness	Growth	Optimism
Challenge	Happiness	Peace
Citizenship	Honesty	Pleasure
Community	Humour	Poise
Compassion	Influence	Popularity
Competency	Inner Harmony	Recognition
Contribution	Justice	Religion
Creativity	Kindness	Reputation

Respect	Service	Success
Responsibility	Spirituality	Trustworthiness
Security	Stability	Wealth
Self-Respect	Status	Wisdom

Note for your journal: Write your answers down in a journal and look at them regularly to remind yourself.

Action: Find your blind spots

How do you find out what you do not know about yourself, in other words, your blind spots?

The answer is: by getting open and honest feedback. Being open to feedback requires adopting a growth mindset. You consider the feedback openly. On the other hand, this does not mean taking every bit of feedback to the letter or personally.

Reflection: Here are the questions you can consider asking yourself:

- Are you open to feedback?
- Are you seriously ready to think about the feedback you receive?
- Are you ready to reflect on the feedback, regardless of where/whom it came from?
- Are you prepared to go back and clarify any unclear items to avoid misunderstanding?

Tips and tools: It is often difficult for people around us to give honest feedback. They might be more comfortable with it if you called it 'opportunities to improve'.

You could ask for feedback from a colleague who knows you and whose opinions you trust. Here is a suggestion: "Hey Martha, I am working on improving a few things about myself in the next year, can you maybe suggest one area I could focus on?"

Note for your journal: Write down your answers to these points in a journal and look at them regularly to remind yourself.

Action: Test your self-awareness

If you would like to test your self-awareness with your colleagues, we have designed a unique self-awareness practice worksheet for you.

Reflection: You can use the 'self-awareness activity' in the next section to ask your colleagues about your Inclusive Intelligence level and start taking action today. Let's be honest now. We all have our own biases one way or another. The most important part of this activity is to reflect on what you learn. Will you be more mindful in your behaviours after your self-discovery?

Tips and tools: Another great tool to help you discover your blind spots is the Harvard Implicit Association Test. It's a free test, anyone can take it online. You can find the link in the References (Project Implicit 2011).

The test has multiple parts. It can be taken against a particular underrepresented group. I often recommend leaders take this test before attending my inclusive leadership session and ask them to share their reflections with me, not the results. Nine out of ten say they are surprised by their results.

Note for your journal: Write down your takeaways from the self-awareness activity. We will have more activities involving them in the next chapter.

Eoin, the manager in the example at the beginning of the chapter, was able to recognise his behaviour in meetings and started using an online feedback tool to give everyone the opportunity to ask questions equally.

FITTING IN MEANS THAT
YOU AS A WHOLE ARE NOT
WELCOMED. YOUR ACCEPTANCE
IS CONDITIONAL AND NOT EVEN
GUARANTEED. FITTING IN IS NOT
FAIR, NOT CONSIDERATE, NOT
INCLUSIVE AND NOT SUSTAINABLE.

Authenticity

1998. Late afternoon. Göztepe, Istanbul. Two people I trust and look up to were fighting about me: my father and my uncle. Two well-educated, middle-aged, authentic men. Their views about the world and lifestyles were completely different but they shared the same blood, assertiveness and obstinacy.

It all started when I showed them the magazine *North West Wind* (the name comes from my surname 'Karayel' in English) I had designed and in which I had edited news from around the world, tech news and personal development tips all by myself using only my own small resources and no internet. I was about 13 or 14 years old and the magazine was all in English, a language I had only been getting familiar with over the last few years.

After a few moments of smiles on both faces, my uncle thought it was the best time to share the truth with me, bluntly. "Furkan, I know you are a talented young girl; I know there is a bright future ahead of you, but have you ever seen a woman leader wearing a headscarf at the head of a big corporate company?" He named two renowned corporate companies in Turkey. "It's always been like this. It will not change. You will end up working in the corner. Why are you giving them a reason not to choose you? You are limiting your own employment options."

These unexpected comments came as a blow to my young self with low self-esteem. It even made me regret showing them what I had done. Selfish me. I had been anticipating praise, not this. As I always do, I winked my right eye and thought for a while.

After careful consideration, I got worried. My uncle was right: I had never seen a woman who looked like me in a leadership position. Not only that, but I was planning a career in tech, a highly male-dominated industry. I was trying to find an answer in my mind, not for my uncle but for myself. I found nothing to say but my worry ignited a fire inside me.

Then my father spoke. He replied to my uncle, saying that, "Furkan can only work for one company at a time. If that company is not happy about how she thinks, what she believes or how she looks despite her incredible skills, that is not a good company anyway and it does not deserve her contributions. This will be a win for Furkan, not a loss." My father's words made so much sense to me, and poured cold water into my internal fire. That's how I learned what authenticity is and what it means to me.

Authenticity is understanding your own core values, what defines you as a person, and living your values to be at your best. Authenticity means finding and being the real you.

For example, respect is one of my core values. I look at the world through this 'filter' to determine whether a situation is respectful or not. Do I show respect for others when facilitating a workshop or meeting with my friend? This is the question that spins in my mind. For me, authenticity means displaying that value of 'respect' for others while living the 'respect' inside me at the same time.

Inclusive leaders are authentic leaders too. They are aware of their true self. Their actions and behaviour reflect their core values.

Bill George said of authentic leaders in his book *True North: Discover Your Authentic Leadership* that they (authentic leaders) "reframe their life stories to understand who they were in the core. In doing so, they discovered the purpose of their leadership and learned that authentic made them more effective" (George 2015).

When a leader is inclusive as well as authentic, it encourages employees and other team leaders in the organisation to bring their authentic self to work, build trust and increase loyalty and productivity.

When authenticity meets inclusion, amazing things happen.

I have not seen many authentic, inclusive leaders in my career in tech. However, my inclusive leadership advisor role has given me opportunities to meet and chat with many such leaders, and to understand their leadership styles as well as their motivators, actions and behaviours.

Cervantes's fictional character Don Quixote is the first person who comes to my mind when I think of authenticity. It was my favourite book from an early age because I could relate to him.

I like how Don Quixote always went to great lengths to challenge the status quo and be an authentic leader in his world. He was relentless in fighting to live by his values despite being perceived as a loser.

I have strong values at my core too. Being a highly sensitive person, authenticity is like breathing to me. Without it, I cannot thrive. It would destroy my self-image and I would lose my belief in myself. Guess what? I am not alone. This applies to all of us – every team and every organisation, anywhere in the world.

Fitting in

It is not always easy to live fully with our authentic self at work because, as employees, we are expected to 'fit in' with the current organisational culture.

Fitting in is the opposite of authenticity. It means you are expected to change to be able to work. It means that you as a whole are not welcomed. Your acceptance is conditional and not even guaranteed.

Fitting in is like giving the same shoes to everyone, men, women, children, seniors, disabled people and more and expecting them to walk and be productive in those shoes all day long. Fitting in is not fair, not considerate, not inclusive and not sustainable.

In terms of my own experience, I tried to bring my authentic self to work every morning. Some days I was successful, some days I was not.

Sometimes, being the only introvert, the only Muslim, the only one from a different background and the only female software engineer on the team – in a highly male-dominated environment too – as well as the only woman with a headscarf in the entire company challenged my self-confidence and put pressure on me to consistently try to adapt. This is emotional labour and emotionally exhausting. Even as I write about it now I can feel the pain in my shoulders.

Leadership was defined in my mind for so many years as "leading and managing large corporate teams in large organisations". Therefore, I never considered myself as a leader, but the Don Quixote inside of me was bouncing from time to time.

It came out one night when I saw another PR article by a large company that was using diversity and inclusion as a marketing tool yet again. At the time I was sitting on my sofa on a night of the holy month of Ramadan, but I immediately stood up. I felt physical pain from frustration in my shoulders again. I needed to do something about it. I did not know what to do, but I knew that if I tried, things could only get better. I could not see the end of the tunnel; it was dark and unknown. But I wanted to embark on the journey anyway.

And so Diversein was born. While I was hungry to learn more about diversity and inclusion, there were so many lessons from my own experiences in the workplace that I could share. I started blogging and sharing diversity inclusion articles, brought together experts in this matter under one roof and have ended up organising so many brilliant events in and out of Ireland.

Yes, this was truly me to the core. I was so happy to do this for people who needed to open up conversations on diversity and inclusion in the workplace, get an opportunity to talk about their authentic self and finally take action on diversity and inclusion. My energy was fuelled by my passion. Finally, I could match my actions and behaviours to my authentic self and become more effective in the world in this way.

8th March 2019. We had organised a women in leadership session, but this time it was different. As I was listening to the amazing trainer Dawn Leane, my mouth dropped: on one of her slides, she had my photo. Dawn referred to me as a leader. "Furkan is a leader who inspires organisations and leaders to take action on diversity and inclusion. She did not have role models growing up," Dawn added. Then she challenged the status quo: "You cannot be, you cannot see."

I was surprised to see this, to be honest. As I mentioned earlier, I have never seen myself as a leader, because I do not match the definition of leadership I had in my mind. Then I came across another definition of leadership by Bill George that made so much sense to me:

"Some leaders did not see themselves as leaders at all. Instead, they wanted to make a difference and inspire others to join them in pursuing common goals. If that isn't leadership, what is?"

Bill George, 2015

4.48am, 21st January 2020. Plano, Texas. It is a cold and still dark morning as I finish writing this chapter. But the Don Quixote inside me is bouncing around in the warm Andalucia desert and "dreaming the impossible dream".

Summary

Inclusive Leaders start the inclusion journey by looking at themselves. They clearly know their core values, motivators and passion. They are open. They look for ways to discover their own blind spots and reflect on their behaviours. They lead with their authenticity.

Activity: Self-awareness

This example for self-awareness practice for the purposes of Inclusive Intelligence aims to bring awareness of the inclusive leadership skills, discover the unknowns about your understanding of the skills and take action to improve them.

1. Rate yourself on how well you practise inclusive leadership traits by filling in the Self-Rating column on the Rating Form, with '1' being the lowest score and '10' the highest.
2. Print several copies of the Individual Feedback Form and hand them out to at least five people you have worked with and whose opinion you trust.
3. Collect the Individual Feedback Forms in a box or envelope so that you cannot associate the feedback with any specific person.
4. Review the Individual Feedback Forms and calculate the average rating you received for each skill. For example, let's say you were rated 4, 7, 8, 5 and 6 for empathy. Add those numbers up and divide the total by the number of people you gave the form to – in this case, the ratings add up to 30 and you had five answers, so your average rating is 30/5 = 6.
5. Write that number in the middle column for that skill on the Rating Form.

6. Then calculate the difference between your self-rating (left column) and the average rating received from others (middle column) and write it down in the Score (Delta) column (right column) on the Rating Form.

7. Highlight the highest numbers in the Score column (right column) on the Rating Form. These are your blind points (negative numbers) or hidden points (positive numbers).

8. Check your self-awareness level using the Analysis File.

9. On the Reflection Form, write down the highest numbers you highlighted in step 7 and write down the actions you should take towards each of them.

See the example filled-out forms provided.

Rating Form – Self-Awareness Practice for Inclusive Intelligence:

	Self-Rating [1 to 10]	Average of Others' Ratings (Take an average of 5 people's ratings about you) [1 to 10]	Score (Delta: Self-rating – Others' ratings)
Empathy			
Engagement			
Commitment			
Vision			
Accountability			
Courage			
Curiosity			
Cultural Intelligence			
Mentorship			
Allyship			
Role Modeling			
Respect			
Resilience			
Transparency			
Recognition & Rewarding			
Adaptability			
Flexibility			
Authenticity			
Other:			

Analysis File – Self-Awareness Practice for Inclusive Intelligence

	Known to Self	Not known to Self
Known to Others	Open	Blind Spot
Not known to Others	Hidden	Unknown

Johari Window (Luft, 1969)

Open – If the difference between your self-rating and ratings by others is zero, then you are a highly self-aware and open leader. You are honest with yourself and others about your strengths and weaknesses. You are open-minded. You welcome feedback as you receive it and are likely to give feedback to others to help them grow.

Hidden – If the difference between your self-rating and ratings by others consists mostly of positive numbers, it means you are highly known to self but not to others. Your skills might be underestimated by your peers because they are hidden and not clearly demonstrated. You can go back to the people who filled out the Rating Form and ask them what made them think so. Start with the ones with whom the difference is highest.

Unknown – This represents information you and others are unaware of.

Blind spot – If the difference between your self-rating and ratings by others mostly consists of negative values, it means the opinion others have of you differs from what you think about yourself. Give yourself enough time to consider what they think, then ask for details in order to clearly understand the problem. Ask for specific examples. Would you still rate yourself the same after listening to the examples? Focus on the highest negative numbers first. How would you reflect on them on a daily basis?

Reflection Form – Self-Awareness Practice for Inclusive Intelligence

List your scores (Delta: your rating – rating by others) from highest to lowest.

Areas to improve	Start doing...	Frequency (daily, weekly, monthly)	Avoid doing
1.			
2.			
3.			

Sample message for sending out the Individual Feedback Form

Dear colleague, I am… … … … …

To become a more effective leader/team member, I am practising Self-Awareness for Inclusive Intelligence. Having worked with you, I would appreciate it if you could share with me the areas you believe I should focus on this year in order to improve.

Thank you for your time.

Level of strength (Circle the number)

Empathy	1	2	3	4	5	6	7	8	9	10
Engagement	1	2	3	4	5	6	7	8	9	10
Commitment	1	2	3	4	5	6	7	8	9	10
Vision	1	2	3	4	5	6	7	8	9	10
Accountability	1	2	3	4	5	6	7	8	9	10
Courage	1	2	3	4	5	6	7	8	9	10
Curiosity	1	2	3	4	5	6	7	8	9	10
Cultural Intelligence	1	2	3	4	5	6	7	8	9	10
Mentorship	1	2	3	4	5	6	7	8	9	10
Allyship	1	2	3	4	5	6	7	8	9	10
Role Modeling	1	2	3	4	5	6	7	8	9	10
Respect	1	2	3	4	5	6	7	8	9	10
Resilience	1	2	3	4	5	6	7	8	9	10
Transparency	1	2	3	4	5	6	7	8	9	10
Recognition & Rewarding	1	2	3	4	5	6	7	8	9	10
Adaptability	1	2	3	4	5	6	7	8	9	10
Flexibility	1	2	3	4	5	6	7	8	9	10
Authenticity	1	2	3	4	5	6	7	8	9	10
Other:	1	2	3	4	5	6	7	8	9	10

Final thoughts:

Example – Rating Form Self-Awareness Practice for Inclusive Intelligence:

	Self-Rating [1 to 10]	Average of Others' Ratings (Take an average of 5 people's ratings about you) [1 to 10]	Score (Delta: Self-rating – Others' ratings)
Empathy	8	2	6
Engagement	10	9	1
Commitment	9	7	2
Vision	4	3	1
Accountability	5	5	0
Courage	5	6	-1
Curiosity	6	6	0
Cultural Intelligence	4	1	3
Mentorship	3	5	-2
Allyship	3	3	0
Role Modeling	6	2	4
Respect	10	4	6
Resilience	7	5	2
Transparency	5	1	4
Recognition & Rewarding	10	4	6
Adaptability	7	3	4
Flexibility	5	4	1
Authenticity	7	3	4
Other:			

Example – Reflection form Self-Awareness for Inclusive Intelligence

Areas to improve	Start doing...	Frequency (daily, weekly, monthly)	Avoid doing
1. Empathy	I will have a one-to-one meeting to understand the needs of my team members coming back from maternity/paternity leave to make them active team members again.	Occasionally	I will not forget to have follow ups after the initial meeting and check with them at a frequency we both agree.
2. Respect	I'll make sure to listen to everybody's opinion in daily meetings.	Daily	I'll make sure I will not speak over anybody and let them finish their sentences.
3. Recognition & Rewarding	I will start writing a thank you email weekly and share with the team to recognise high achievers.	Weekly	I will not forget to include team enablers who support others to achieve in the team.

Interview with Asif Sadiq MBE, Head of Equity and Inclusion, International at WarnerMedia

Furkan Karayel: What does self-awareness mean for an inclusive leader?

Asif Sadiq MBE: It is important for truly inclusive leaders to showcase a new leadership style, one that shows vulnerability, authentic engagement and the eagerness to listen and understand. The changing world around us has showcased to many leaders that we can no longer replicate our companies' Diversity and Inclusion vision. We all need to go on a journey of discovery to find our personal 'why' in order to authentically champion change.

Leaders must create psychological safety for themselves and those around them to create environments where teams can learn and grow together through exploring difference and creating understanding to achieve common objectives that accelerate cultural change within an organisation.

Doing this also requires us to be critical of ourselves and aware of our biases and privilege in order to be able to implement change. The most important thing for any leader to understand is that they must go into conversations with an open mind to create meaningful dialogue that can drive change. There isn't a magic formula for this or a textbook way of doing it: what is key is that leaders do it authentically, utilising their personal leadership style.

Self-awareness requires us to reflect on our behaviours and leadership style to see what we can change to become an authentic human leader. Workplaces of the future will require leaders to think inclusively, act inclusively and, above all else, learn inclusively. Being consciously inclusive and aware of our actions will help us in creating workplaces that are not only inclusive of everyone but are also successful.

What is your takeaway from this chapter?

If you reflect on and share your learnings regularly, they stay in your memory longer and you start internalising them.

Reflect and share your learning experience below.

Please also feel free to share personal experiences of inclusion and diversity.

WE CANNOT EMPATHISE WITH SOMEONE IF WE HAVE A BIAS AGAINST THEM.

CHAPTER TWO:

EMPATHY

Introduction

Does empathy matter at work? Or is it overrated?

In this chapter, we will be looking at the place of empathy in Inclusive Intelligence. We will talk about what empathy means at work and whether it really matters.

You will also find practical actions with real stories in this section.

Let's get started.

"In the past, jobs were about muscles, now they are about brains, but in the future, they will be about the heart."

Minouche Shafik

'What are the characteristics of an inclusive leader?' We posed this question to our Inclusive Leadership workshop participants. A large number of them said 'openness' and 'empathy'.

No surprise! According to recent studies empathy is one of the core leadership skills. Empathy improves productivity, employee retention and engagement in the workplace (Sinar et al. 2016).

Brené Brown describes empathy as "simply listening, holding space, withholding judgment, emotionally connecting, and communicating that incredibly healing message of 'you're not alone.'" (Brown 2015)

Empathy is also a key component of Emotional Intelligence (Goleman 2005).

Today only 40 per cent of business leaders have strong empathy skills and companies have already started to invest a significant number of resources into building empathy skills in the workplace (Sinar et al. 2016).

Silvija Delekovcan, Human Resources Leader, shares her experience with empathy: "I learned about the power of empathy in leadership in my early twenties through charity and community work. To make things happen with no monetary resources (and without much experience behind me), I realised that I could only do so by getting the buy-in of those who had the skills and keeping them motivated. This meant learning what makes each individual tick – this is where empathy came into play.

"It was only a decade later that I learned about the importance of self-empathy in leadership. As a leader, being empathetic to others is not enough. As with all other leadership virtues, empathy in leadership is effective only if genuine and authentic – it has to be exercised with oneself first. Otherwise, it leads to burnout. A daily reflection practice and self-compassion helps me to create more capacity for those around me, keep my fire lit, and makes me a better human."

Before talking about the three types of leadership when it comes to empathy, let me be clear that there is no right or wrong in empathy, like in most things in life. Our behaviours may sometimes demonstrate more empathy, sometimes not.

Everyone's condition, life experiences and environment are completely different. What I am trying to ask you here is to look at your daily actions to decide whether you consider them empathetic and how can you move closer to empathy one step at a time.

There are three types of leaders when it comes to empathy:

1- Naturally Empathetics: They are the people who have empathy built into their core identity. They make decisions with their empathy. At work, they are recognised as highly approachable.

You see these leaders mentoring junior employees. They emphasise and reflect on their experiences through the mentee's point of view.

Empathetic leaders often use these sentences:

- "I hear you."
- "I would feel the same as you are feeling now."
- "Please tell me more about it."
- "In those times, doing X helped me. Do you think it may help you too?"
- "I am here if I can be any help."

2- Underestimaters: These managers do not specifically pay attention to other people's feelings and they do not see it as an issue.

Research by the University of California shows that increased power lowers the ability to read emotions and the ability to adapt behaviours to others (Keltner 2016).

Empathy requires us to see each other first and accept each other as our authentic selves. We cannot empathise with people if we have a bias against them. Therefore, by practising empathy, we can break the ice, challenge our unconscious bias and break the stereotypes in our minds.

3- Adaptables: These are the leaders who do not automatically empathise with their colleagues but are aware of their behaviours and open to change. Research shows that empathy is a learnable skill, rather than a trait (Pounds 2014).

Going back to the 'self-awareness first' rule, which of these examples resonates with you more? Would you call yourself a naturally empathetic leader? What do your colleagues say about it?

If you are recognised as an empathetic leader, happy days!

If not, here are some steps you can take.

Action: Start with curiosity

Empathy starts with curiosity and the courage to know the other person. Without knowing the other person and understanding their values and motivators, it is just a failed good intention.

Reflection: Give yourself time to think about and acknowledge:

- How well do you know your colleagues?
- How often do you empathise with them and in what situations?

- Do you empathise with the ones you know better?

Tips and tools: My friend, a mother of three working in a corporate job, complained to me once that she was not invited to a late social activity by her team because it was assumed that she would not be able to make it anyway.

As an inclusive leader working in a multicultural environment, empathy is strongly linked to cultural wisdom which is the courage to get an understanding of various cultures and being sensitive to their values and open to meeting people from a different cultural background. We will discuss this further in the cultural wisdom module.

Note for your journal: Write your answers down in a journal and look at them regularly to remind yourself.

Action: Behaviours are contagious

Behaviours are contagious and they make our culture.

Reflection: Share your empathy publicly first and then help to build an empathy culture.

Tips and tools: Can you recognise empathy in these sentences?

- Susan, I don't want you to work on this project this week.

OR

- Susan, I am conscious that you haven't taken the online marketing training yet, so I don't expect you to operate on this project until you fully complete it.

In the first example, Susan has no idea why she is not included in the project whereas in the second one she knows why. In addition to this, she appreciates the empathy shown here that keeps her from working on something that she is not yet ready to take on.

Action: Look for empathy in new hires

As an inclusive leader, you are also accountable for recognising and rewarding empathetic behaviours in your team that will motivate others and eventually build a more empathetic work environment. So, it makes sense to look for this new skill in your talent candidates.

Reflection: Why not add an extra step to your interview questions to understand the candidate's empathy level?

ALLYSHIP IS THE COURAGE TO CHOOSE CARING FOR PEOPLE WHO DON'T LOOK LIKE YOU.

Allyship

In diversity and inclusion conversations, we also often hear the word 'allyship'.

Allyship is empathising with and understanding the experiences of other underrepresented groups and advocating with them to tackle their needs. Allyship is the courage to choose caring for people who don't look like you.

Here are some examples of allyship:

- Attending an event aimed at tackling the difficulties experienced by people of colour in the workplace.
- Listening to educational content like podcast series or online courses to understand the needs of a disabled person in the workplace.
- Asking your trans team member on the first day at work how you can make it easy for them.

Inclusive leaders practise allyships for all underrepresented groups and they do not favour one group over the others. I often witness a common behaviour that diversity is limited to gender perspective. When they say 'diversity', some people actually only refer to 'gender equality'.

Last year, I had the opportunity to listen to the amazing Dr Ebun Joseph, author of the book *Critical Race Theory and Inequality in the labour market. Racial stratification in Ireland* and expert on Black Studies. Dr Ebun Joseph referred to this as 'Creating inclusion with taste base'.

She mentioned that unfortunately the concepts of diversity and inclusion are sometimes limited by people's choice. It could be gender-specific only or race-specific only, and so on. This is why YOUR definition of diversity and inclusion matters. We must all work to break this narrative and expand the meaning of diversity.

Summary

Empathy is putting yourself in the shoes of others and it is the most important skill for an inclusive leader. You can start testing your own behaviours and practising where you can implement it in your daily activities.

Allyship is empathising with people from underrepresented groups and advocating with them on their needs.

Mentoring junior employees and having more conversations with people from underrepresented groups to understand their views are good practices for empathy and allyship.

Activity: Empathy for Inclusive Intelligence

At the end of group session meetings with your direct reports, use a meeting interaction tool and ask the team to rate the empathy and inclusion level of the meeting. They can access the link on their mobile phones and rate the meeting anonymously.

You can use mentimeter.com, which is a free and easy-to-use meeting engagement tool to interact with the audience in seconds.

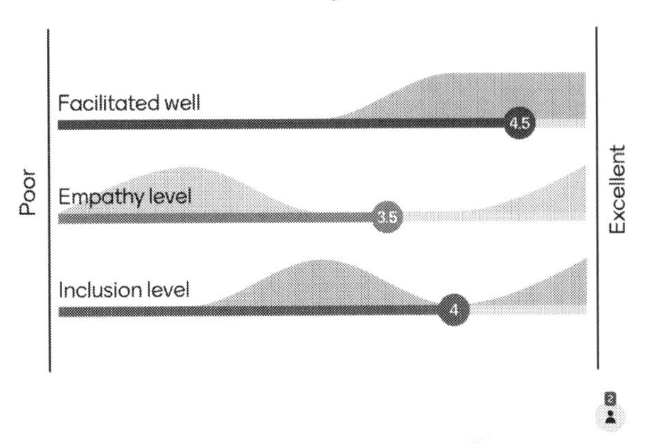

Interview with Aldagh McDonogh, board member at Morgan McKinley

Furkan Karayel: Aldagh, in our course we talk about the importance of inclusive leadership and we summarise it in six pillars: self-awareness, empathy, engagement, cultural wisdom, accountability and commitment. In your own words, what do you think are the most important skills of inclusive leadership, and why?

Aldagh McDonogh: When I started to look at this recently, obviously the first thing you do is you start to look for a definition and there were just so many definitions of inclusive leadership around, but what I found was that they all centred around relationships and valuing personal differences, and that really resonated with me and I thought it's a good, simple summary of what the definition might be.

So, really, for me, I think the most important skill for inclusive leadership is that you actively seek out those differences and don't just wait for them to appear. I mean, it's one level of inclusive leadership to say "oh, actually there's a different point of view", but to actually seek it out is a different level, I think, and that's one of the differences in a strong inclusive leader.

I think it can be time-consuming to do that, I think it can be slower in a way and in business we like to move through things quickly, so I do think it can be challenging to execute and to live inclusive leadership versus just agreeing with the theory of it.

I do think it's about actively seeking it out and I suppose really making sure that you're in the position to do that, and to do that you need to build a diverse team in the first place so that you have a greater opportunity of hearing different views, and then making sure that you're protecting yourself from the bias that you inevitably carry.

So you have to be really active in seeking out different views, I think. That's the number one skill that'll set you on the right path, I think, for being more inclusive.

FK: Thank you very much, this is a very important point, as you said, and when it comes to empathy, Aldagh, research shows that empathy is one of the most important skills for leadership, and in business at the moment leaders don't have empathy skills. I've seen that you achieved this, so what do you think leaders should do to be able to gain empathy skills?

AMcD: First of all, thank you very much for your kind words. I'm really pleased that you felt that because I think, particularly with mentoring, you're there to help understand the person's situation and come up and help them with what they can do from where they are, so empathy I think is key in that.

But one of the things I just say on empathy first of all, and I think it might be one of the reasons why people don't practise it, or if you're saying that the research says that they don't practise it, maybe the reason is that empathy, I think, can sometimes be confused with having to do what the other person's view is, or having to actually move in that direction, but for me that's not the case at all.

What empathy is, is that you have to hear the point of view and consider it and then come to your own conclusion and that's a big difference, whereas sometimes people can feel that people who are very empathetic have no voice or no view of their own and I think that's completely wrong.

I think some of the other things for consideration around empathy are that you have to, I believe, believe that you're not the only leader in the room, you're not the only expert in the room, that you've got to value the other perspectives.

Then you take the time to actually inquire about them and to understand where the other person's coming from. I think you have to ask open questions because otherwise you can't really understand where the other person is in the discussion, or in the issue or in the problem.

I think wherever possible, and maybe it's my marketing background, my brand building background, but walking in your customers' or your team's shoes, spending the time doing what they do if you can, or at least really working to try and understand it is critical because then their input or their position becomes much more understandable.

I think coming away from the workplace maybe for a minute, I think things like traveling massively builds your empathy skills because you experience different perspectives of the world, of everything from how people travel, how they live, how they eat, and it does make you think about the other people's approaches to the same things and why that is.

Read a different newspaper. I've recently started to try and force myself to do this, and to listen to and read other people's views on things that I know I don't agree with, and it's really hard going but if you want to understand it then you have to put yourself in the position of that and actually what it's doing is building my empathy skills.

I still come back to my first point, which is that it doesn't mean that you have to take that person's position on board, but you absolutely should consider it as an inclusive leader with empathy.

FK: Very good points. I really like the way that you talked about reading through other people's opinions and asking open-ended questions as you said with traveling, understanding different views and considering that you are not the only leader. All of those are really important for empathy and inclusive leadership.

What is your takeaway from this chapter?

If you reflect and share your learnings regularly, they stay in your memory longer and you start internalising them.

Reflect and share your learning experience below.

EMOTIONAL INVESTMENT IS THE INVESTMENT OF YOUR ENERGY AND TIME INTO BUILDING A RELATIONSHIP WITH SOMEONE ELSE EITHER IN A PERSONAL OR PROFESSIONAL CONTEXT.

CHAPTER THREE: **ENGAGEMENT**

Introduction

Welcome back. So far, we have covered the self-awareness and empathy pillars of Inclusive Intelligence. Self-awareness and empathy are also elements of Emotional Intelligence and fall under both disciplines.

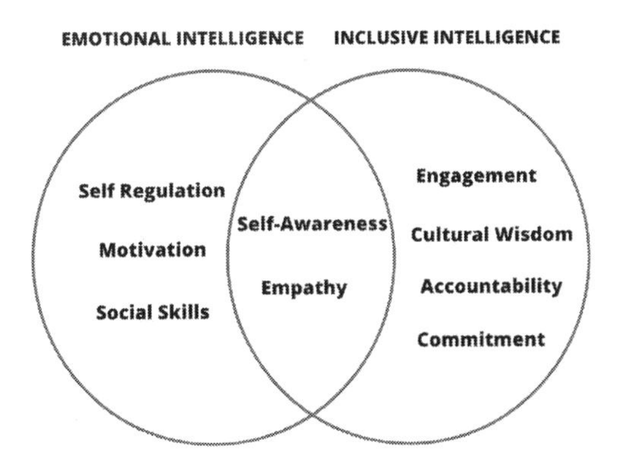

In this chapter, we will dive deep into engagement. Both at the employee and at the team level. How does engagement impact your team's overall success? We will look at examples from real-life stories and very simple actions that you can take to keep your team engaged.

Let's get started.

"Coming together is a beginning, staying together is progress, and working together is success."

Henry Ford

Archana was the founder of a tech startup based in India. One day, she announced that she could no longer pay her employees and she had to make them redundant. However, Archana's employees had a strong bond with her. Shockingly, they refused to leave the company and continued working with her for half of their pay. A few years later, Hubbl was sold for millions of dollars. One of the employees explained that "Archana knew everyone in the office. She had a personal relationship with each one of us. She did not get upset when we made mistakes but gave us the time to learn how to analyse and fix the situation." (Seppälä 2014).

What we see here is that Archana has mastered employee engagement. She shows care openly. She is thoughtful. More importantly, she is a human being like all of us. She makes mistakes too. But her genuine engagement and collaboration with her employees on a human level paid off during her most challenging times.

Is your team truly engaged? Employee engagement rate stands at only 15 per cent globally (Gallup 2017). In other words, companies only get 15 per cent productivity from their workforces.

To be honest, when I think of this global engagement rate, it frustrates me so much. Let me be clear, I am not frustrated with the people who perform at 15 per cent at work. I am frustrated with the leaders who don't invest the time to understand who their team members truly are, what's going on in their lives and what their motivators are.

This is called emotional investment and means that you invest your energy and time into building a relationship with someone else either in a personal or professional context.

Without emotional investment, the workload may turn into pressure and stress. This is not sustainable. When someone is in that situation, they automatically go into 'fight or flight' mode. Most employees choose 'flight' and change company. As mentioned earlier, that is one of the biggest reasons the current employee retention rate is less than two years globally (Peterson 2017).

Employee engagement is the emotional state of an employee, a combination of their openness to building relationship bridges between peers and their trust in the organisation and its goals. In conversations, we refer to engaged employees as 'open' and to unengaged employees as 'closed up'.

Leaders have a big role to play here. With their observations and behaviours, the engagement rate can change dramatically, like in Archana's story.

When I talk about engagement, many people only relate this to quarterly employee performance meetings with managers. To be honest, I am not a big fan of these meetings. I believe it limits your engagement to four hours in a year, maybe even less. You go through a planned agenda and have no time to have deeper conversations about your actual goals, how you want to achieve them and what support your manager can give you.

I am not surprised that I am not alone in this. Some organisations don't bother with annual reviews anymore. Instead, they adopt instant feedback and hand out small weekly bonuses to employees they see doing well.

There are many forms of engagement that can help inclusive leaders.

Action: Measure and monitor engagement

The first step to employee engagement can be understanding where your team or organisation stands on engagement.

Reflection: Measure and monitor under what circumstances your team's engagement rises or falls so you can take further actions to tackle lack of engagement.

Tips and tools: Have you tried an employee engagement tool or application before? It's definitely worth considering. You can find some examples by clicking on the link in the References and Further Reading section (Heinz 2021).

Action: Know your team members personally

Inclusive leaders are accountable for getting their team members to engage and deliver great products and results. In order to be able to achieve this, inclusive leaders must know their team members, their values, motivators and preferences. We touched on this in the Empathy section in more detail.

Reflection: Consider a person from your team you know the least about. You can invite him/her 15 minutes early to your one-on-one meetings (for example, their annual review meeting) to have some time for a casual chat and to get to know each other.

During my online lectures, I implemented this method for my classes at the Equality, Diversity and Inclusion Master's module at Dún Laoghaire Institute of Art, Design + Technology. It definitely gave me an opportunity to connect with the students before class and to have casual conversations we all missed so much when doing online classes.

Tips and tools: Consider Ellen. She invited her team to dinner at a famous steak house in town to celebrate the team's success. Vegan team members were not happy with this and found a reason not to attend. It had never occurred to Ellen never that her way of rewarding the team was not inclusive.

Note for your journal: Write your answers down in a journal and look at them regularly to remind yourself.

Action: Interactive sessions for feedback and recognition

Feedback is a great way to engage with the team and the team members together. Having said that, inclusive leaders need to build an environment where feedback is constructive and appreciated.

Reflection: Why not?

Book a reminder on your team members' agenda for the team to take 15 minutes on Friday afternoons to write down their 'thank you' messages to other members who helped them to get the work done that week. It may be on a communication channel that is open to all members. This will motivate the team members to engage more with each other, as well as increase communication and productivity.

Tips and tools: I worked for a company for five years, mostly in the same department. By the end of my time with them, I attended a training course where I was sitting next to one of my team members with whom I had not had many conversations (remember I am an introvert). During that interactive training course, I learned more about him than in five years of conversations. After that training, I was able to communicate with him more easily.

Action: Mentorship

Mentorship is my favourite engagement method. I call it an opportunity to have an impact on another life. Our journeys in our personal life and career are like our fingerprints. They are all unique. They are full of wisdom to reflect on. In fact, mentorship is a two-way street. You learn and share at the same time.

Reflection: As an inclusive leader, you can choose to either initiate or be part of an internal/external mentorship programme to truly engage with your team members and emerging aspiring inclusive leaders, and understand different perspectives.

If you don't have a mentor, it is better to ask a peer you feel close to and whose feedback and contribution to your growth you can appreciate.

Tips and tools: Mentorship works best when you can relate to your mentor. That's why programmes involving women helping other women are so successful. People sharing relatively similar backgrounds or values can better understand each other's challenges and can are better able to help.

During my early career, I had great mentors. One of them was Grace. She started her career one year before me. She was my go-to person if I had any problems. She knew me, my values, personality and where I was on my journey so her mentorship added so much value to my career growth.

Summary

Leaders' observations and behaviour play a big role in increasing employee engagement and maximising team potential. Measuring and monitoring engagement rate, investing quality time into one-to-one conversations, introducing mentoring and interactive sessions for feedback and recognition are some of the steps inclusive leaders can take to build an engaged culture.

Activity: Engagement activity

When your team members socialise together, their engagement level moves to the next level. It's an opportunity for them to show who they are as a person outside of work and that's where the real connection happens. My favourite way of socialising as a team is through corporate social responsibility projects.

Select a community activity or corporate social responsibility (CSR) project as a team and regularly participate in that activity together. Here are some examples:

- Helping local students or senior citizens to gain certain skills.
- Volunteering for non-profit organisation activities such as climate change or homelessness.
- Joining a charity walk.
- Volunteering at mental health or wellbeing awareness activities.

What is your takeaway from this chapter?

If you reflect and share your learnings regularly, they stay in your memory longer and you start internalising them.

Reflect and share your learning experience below.

WHEN STEREOTYPE IS TAKEN INTO A BEHAVIOUR OR A VERBAL EXPRESSION, IT BECOMES A MICROAGGRESSION.

CHAPTER FOUR: **CULTURAL WISDOM**

Introduction

Culture… a word that conveys so much: similarities, differences or harmony.

What about cultural wisdom? Have you heard this expression before? In this chapter you will read an interesting story from my personal experience to illustrate what we mean by cultural wisdom and how you can develop your own cultural wisdom using simple actions.

Let's do it.

"Culture eats strategy for breakfast."

Peter Drucker

Years ago, I used to work for a multinational telecom company. On the warmest days of Irish summer, the company ordered an ice cream van to enable the employees to enjoy the sunshine outside. It was the first day of Ramadan and I was fasting. But it really was fine with me. I didn't mind it at all. I was at my desk and working away as usual. However, this experience eventually became so frustrating for me. Let me tell you why.

Each person passing by my desk was asking me why I was not eating an ice cream. Some said "Furkan, come on. Go and get one". I had to explain myself to so many people that afternoon and it was very exhausting emotionally. As I repeated myself over and over again, I started to feel more deeply that afternoon like the company I worked for didn't care about me and my choice. While the rest of the employees' energy level went up, mine went down.

Let me be clear again. Everyone's intention was good. I really did appreciate the people who thought of me and stopped by my desk. They wanted me to get the best out of this experience. I was even feeling good about my response to each of them.

However, I later felt the heaviness of the emotional labour and could not even understand the reason why I was feeling that way. It took me some time to reach a conclusion. It was daunting. It was definitely not easy. But it was there.

Cultural wisdom means having a curiosity towards different cultures, respecting their points of view, daring to learn from differences with an open mindset and integrating cultural intelligence in a way that creates harmony in the team/organisation.

Cultural intelligence is the core element of cultural wisdom. It is defined by David Livermore in his book *Leading with Cultural Intelligence* as the "capability to function effectively across national, ethnic, and organisational cultures."

The world is small today. We travel overseas more (this sentence was obviously written pre-Covid times!), we do more business with companies on a global scale. The number of multicultural teams increases every day. Consequently, cultural wisdom has a huge impact on increasing team performance, talent retention and the feeling of belonging.

Did you know that 70 per cent of international ventures continue to fail because of cultural differences (Livermore 2009)?

Last year, I asked my social media followers if their managers were familiar with their background culture. Seventy-eight per cent of them said "no". It is very obvious that most managers are missing a huge opportunity to get the most out of their employees.

How do you develop/demonstrate cultural wisdom in your workplace?

Let's consider practical steps you can take.

Action: Be open, create channels for communication and feedback

Tips and tools: In my 'ice cream' story I knew that my company was not aware of how I, as someone from another culture, was not able to join in the social activity. If my manager had known, I am sure they would definitely have done their best to include me. The problem was that they had no open doors for me or other people to bring an issue like this to them.

Reflection: Reflect on how you can put this into practice.

What channels for communication and feedback can you create? How do you make sure everyone knows about these channels? What have you tried previously? Do they email you to bring any issues like this? Do they choose to talk to you in person?

Note for your journal: Write your answers down in a journal and look at them regularly to remind yourself.

Action: Actively look for opportunities to learn and increase your cultural wisdom

Look for opportunities to increase your cultural intelligence level as much as possible. The more you learn about different cultures, the more inclusive you become.

Reflection: Reflect on how you can put this into practice.

Maybe you could celebrate Chinese New Year with your team members, or Pride Parade or Ramadan dinners? What other actions can you take? What other things have you tried with your team that have worked well?

Note for your journal: Write your answers down in a journal and look at them regularly to remind yourself.

Action: Become aware of your blind spots and stereotypes

Inclusive leaders with extensive cultural intelligence do not label or stereotype people as they discover more about a new culture.

Instead, inclusive leaders know that every single person, with their experiences and personalities, is different. Cultural intelligence gives inclusive leaders a better bigger picture to understand the truth of that person.

When we see someone for the first time, we form a judgment about them in seconds based on how they look, our social norms, our intuition and our past experiences. Then we put them into either in-groups or out-groups.

We unconsciously put people into our in-groups if we approve of them or they are familiar to us. On the other hand, we put people into our out-groups if we don't approve of them.

These things happen in our unconscious mind in seconds. We spend less energy and time in our unconscious mind as opposed to our conscious mind because we want to pass judgment as soon as possible. As a result, we develop bias against people when we judge them wrongly. This is called unconscious bias, and sometimes blind spots.

Stereotyping and microaggression

Merriam-Webster describes microaggression as "a comment or action that subtly and often unconsciously or unintentionally expresses a prejudiced attitude toward a member of a marginalised group (such as a racial minority)" (Merriam-Webster n.d.)

Here are some examples of microaggression (Diversein 2021):

- "Where are you really from?"
- "Why do you sound white?"
- "Why is your daughter so white?"
- "You are not really Asian."
- "I do not see you as a black girl."
- "So, you are Chinese, right?"
- "You do not act like a normal black person."
- "You do not wear a headscarf, so you are not Muslim then?"

The list can go on forever. What we see here is putting everyone in a race or culture into the same category without seeing them as individuals. That is stereotyping. When this stereotype is taken into behaviour, it's a microaggression.

For example, when I first moved to Ireland about 16 years ago, many people used to ask me if it was my first time seeing snow or did not expect me to be used to rain. I told them that where I come from in Turkey is the rainiest part of the country and it rains there like in Ireland. When I added that Turkey has a proper winter season with snow as well as hot summers, it changed their views.

Tips and tools: One of my clients told me that he had hired a new employee from Turkey and wanted to make sure he prepared a prayer room before his arrival. He was trying to empathise without cultural intelligence, assuming that all Turks believe in the same religion and practise it daily. I suggested that he could ask whether the new hire required an additional room or facility to meet his needs while working.

Reflection: Reflect on how you can put this into practice.

Action: Build harmony

Let your team increase their cultural intelligence levels and learn from each other.

Tips and tools: Organise team engagement activities or 'lunch and learn' sessions about a culture presented by a team member from a different cultural background specifically aimed at showcasing stereotypes they have faced about their culture. These are great examples for increasing cultural intelligence in the team and building more engagement, harmony and a feeling of belonging.

You don't have to have all the answers. Look for help from your team members. They will be delighted to share their perspectives with you.

Reflection: Show that you are open to learning from different cultures and let them help you with this. An inclusive leader is someone who gives their colleagues the opportunity to understand and help them to become better inclusive leaders.

Before launching my Inclusive Intelligence online course, I had an opportunity to have a business mentor as part of the national Covid response for businesses. I was very excited about this as these had been really challenging times for me.

I was finally assigned to a mentor. When I met him virtually, I told him that I was planning to launch my online course. The first question he asked me was, "Who is going to present the course?" I replied, "I am. Because it's the course and the concept I developed." He then recommended that I get my online courses recorded by someone with a different accent. He added Irish or Canadian accent.

I did not follow this advice, for obvious reasons, as this completely goes against my own values for diversity and inclusion. But the sad fact is that 10 years ago, when my self-confidence was much lower, I would have followed it.

Summary: Inclusive leadership without cultural wisdom is unthinkable. Remember, nobody is born with that. It requires dedicated work indeed. Leaders must look for opportunities to build more personal experiences with different cultures, always be open to embracing different ways of working, avoid stereotyping and microaggressions, and build harmony within their teams out of this richness.

Activity: Culture map exercise

Culture Mapping is a tool designed by Erin Meyer to allow you to easily see the differences between cultures and communicate effectively across different cultures (Meyer 2016). Its methodology is based on the following eight categories:

- Communicating – Are the members of the team low-context (simple, verbose and clear) or high-context (rich, deep meaning in interactions)?
- Evaluating – When giving negative feedback, does one give it directly or prefer being indirect and discreet?
- Persuading – Do they like to hear specific cases and examples or prefer holistic, detailed explanations?
- Leading – Are people in the group egalitarian or do they prefer hierarchy?
- Deciding – Are decisions made by consensus or top-down?
- Trusting – Do people base trust on how well they know each other or how well they work together?
- Disagreeing – Are disagreements tackled directly or do people prefer to avoid confrontations?
- Scheduling – Do they perceive time as absolute linear points or consider it a flexible range?

You can draw a culture map of your team. Instead of focusing on countries, you can focus on each team member's preference to improve your team communication.

Draw a culture map of your team; instead of focusing on countries, you can focus on each team member's preference to improve your team communication.

Explicit .... Communicating .... Implicit

Direct negative feedback..... Evaluating ... Indirect negative feedback

Deductive .... Persuading ....Inductive

Egalitarian..................... Leading .... Hierarchical

Consensual.................. Deciding ....Top-down

Task .... Trusting.................. Relationship

Confrontational............. Disagreeing .... Avoid confrontation

Structured.................. Scheduling .... Flexible

Example usage of culture mapping.

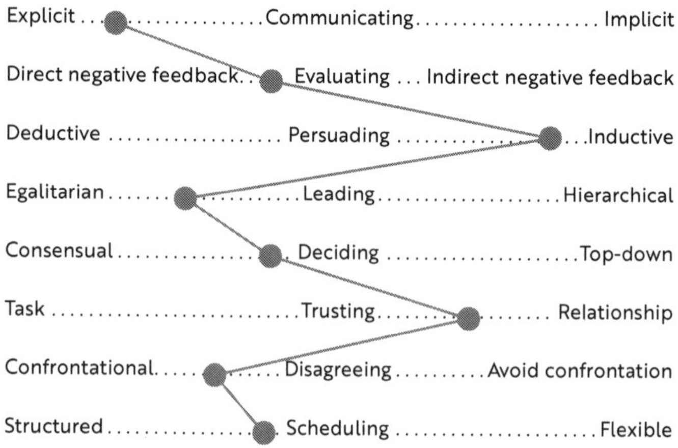

Explicit .... Communicating .... Implicit

Direct negative feedback..... Evaluating ... Indirect negative feedback

Deductive .... Persuading ....Inductive

Egalitarian..................... Leading .... Hierarchical

Consensual.................. Deciding ....Top-down

Task .... Trusting.................. Relationship

Confrontational............. Disagreeing .... Avoid confrontation

Structured.................. Scheduling .... Flexible

Interview with Roxanne Gimbel, systems delivery consultant

Furkan Karayel: Roxanne, could you tell us how you make these personal connections with people/ your clients from very different cultures in such a short time? How did this impact your leadership/ work?

Roxanne Gimbel: Hi. My name is Roxanne Gimbel. For the past 26 years I have lived in the UK and project managed the IT and information portions of engineering projects all over the world.

A former boss once asked me, "What is wrong with you, Roxanne? When I go on a business trip, I might meet a client for a drink, but you get invited to their houses, get involved with them. They even do your laundry!" I was puzzled. At the time, I didn't understand how my way of working with other cultures might be different.

I recently attended a webinar where the presenter stated that *we should treat others the way THEY want to be treated*. I'd like to think this sums up how I've attempted to connect with clients and colleagues across cultures.

Be polite and respectful (the way your mother taught you!).

I try to learn enough of a language to be able to say, "Please", "Thank You", "Hello" and "Goodbye", as well as "How are you today?". Find out how to pronounce and spell your colleagues' names and how they prefer to be addressed. I HATE my name being misspelled or mispronounced, but I make an exception for my Japanese counterparts, who invariably call me Rocky-san-san.

Smile.

A smile is worth a thousand words. While I was in the Forbidden City, a young mother and her two-year-old son were hovering. When I smiled at her, she gestured to me, then her camera and finally her son. I got down on my knees beside her son, she took pictures and all three of us smiled. No words, but instant connection.

Give something of yourself.

Share something about yourself and you will be surprised at what you learn in return. I was in some ancient caves in southern India. I'd acquired an entourage of about 10 children aged 6 to 10 and their parents. The guide tried to shoo them away. A six-year-old spokesman said, "We are learning to speak English. Can we ask you some questions?" "Okay", I said cautiously. Each child had a chance to ask questions like, "Where do you live?" and I learned what these Indian children thought about the world.

Listen to what they say (and what they don't).

It's always important to watch and listen to your team members and clients and what they say, but also what they do not say.

The IT coordinator working for me in a Kuwait project office was becoming distracted and agitated and appeared to have done no preparations for a major office move. When he and I were alone, he began to cry and told me he'd received a letter stating his contract had only been extended for a year. He was the major family breadwinner and was terrified they would be left without income. After I verified his employment, he relaxed and our interactions were better, because he now trusted me enough to be honest with me.

Ask for advice (the laundry story).

One great way to start a dialog with someone new is to ask for advice. This can be something simple, such as where the best local place to go for dinner is.

Frau Weigelt was a client at an East German refinery. She was shy speaking English and, although our conversations in German were fine, she was still hesitant. When I confided I had no place to do laundry, she took my dirty clothes home, washed and ironed them. Over the next six years, we worked productively and shared many insights into East German life and Disney musicals…

Offer assistance.

If you can provide support or information to make team members' or clients' experiences more effective or productive, everyone benefits.

Japanese clients visiting my Canadian office were having spirited discussions in Japanese. I asked if I could help. "What is maple syrup?" one of them asked. "We wish to take some back to Japan." That night, I stopped at a farm stand on my way home and purchased several small tins of maple syrup which I distributed to the class, who were delighted. We were then able to refocus on the course agenda, but our lunchtime conversations still included what maternity leave was and why Canadians don't peel grapes…

Be willing to try something new.

You may occasionally be asked to participate in activities outside your experience or comfort zone. If you respond with good humour, you immediately strengthen your connections.

I was invited to lunch by our Chinese JV partners. The attendees included the IT director, several department managers, an interpreter and me. The lunch took place in a large private dining room in a Beijing restaurant. Before the IT director ordered, he asked through the interpreter, "Is there anything you WON'T eat?" My response was "Feet", which, I explained, I did not eat because "they are too much work for too little meat." Everyone laughed. The food was delicious and the meetings afterwards were productive.

Be patient.

None of this happens instantaneously, so be patient. Time to build connections is different for each culture. In some cultures, the relative time may be equated to water wearing over stones… which we all know can take a while!

How my approach has impacted my work.

We are taught to be formal and 'business-like' in our interactions within a working environment. The difficulty with this in a multicultural setting is that each distinct group may have different ideas of what that actually means, since each culture and each individual is unique.

I have found that my connecting individually to team members and clients builds a cumulative foundation of trust, (hopefully) respect and, most importantly, understanding. This has helped build cohesive teams, improved communications and reduced the potential for misunderstanding and conflict.

What is your takeaway from this chapter?

If you reflect and share your learnings regularly, they stay in your memory longer and you start internalising them.

Reflect and share your learning experience below.

IN INCLUSIVE WORKPLACES, THERE IS NO TOLERANCE FOR PERSONAL ACCUSATIONS AND FINGER POINTING.

CHAPTER FIVE: **ACCOUNTABILITY**

Introduction

Who's accountable for diversity and inclusion in your organisation?

Do you have a diversity and inclusion department managing all the programmes and activities?

Or do you have a team of volunteers who run regular events?

Or are you a small team who does not have anybody in charge of these in your organisation?

Don't worry.

In this chapter you'll learn what accountability means for an inclusive leader; what happens when there is a lack of accountability; what actions can help you develop your accountability for diversity and inclusion; and more.

It's my favourite chapter in this book.

So, let's get started.

"Accountability is a statement of personal promise, both to yourself and to the people around you, to deliver specific defined results."

Brian Dive

"It's not my job!"

We hear this very often when we are not motivated by the end result of an action.

Accountability in Inclusive Intelligence means, regardless of position in an organisation, sharing the diversity and inclusion vision without needing an external force such as another manager or person.

Inclusive leaders are self-motivated and enthusiastic people who want to have an impact on their journey into inclusion. By doing this, they also influence others around them with their decisions and challenge the status quo.

According to the 2017 'The Leadership Accountability Gap' report by Lee Hecht Harrison, 72 per cent of global participants said they believe leadership accountability is a critical business issue. Only 31 per cent of the participants said they were satisfied with the degree of leadership accountability (Molinaro 2017).

As one said, "Great leaders are good human beings too." They genuinely believe that they have a responsibility to make their workplace as inclusive as possible. And they take action to participate in the mission.

Years ago, I was invited to an event and there I spoke with a high-level manager of a Wall Street company. After I introduced myself and my work around diversity and inclusion, he told me his company, which has thousands of employees globally, has no problem with diversity and inclusion in any of their offices in the world. He added, "we have a Human Resources Department. They handle it."

For some people, diversity and inclusion is 'handled' by others and everything looks perfect from their side. Please do let me know if you have seen a 'perfect' organisation. Because after working for many years in many different industries, I still have not.

Diverse background does not equal inclusive mindset

During my 15-year career in the industry, I have seen one mistake repeated over and over again. I call it "inclusion on paper".

All individuals from underrepresented groups are believed to be inclusive by default.

They are also expected to be accountable for diversity and inclusion groups and initiatives in the organisation, and to take the lead and advocate for their differences. Consequently, in some companies, a diverse background employee can be promoted to make numbers look good without anyone understanding whether they have an inclusive mindset. I am sure you are familiar with "women block women" or "similar background people block each other's progress" stories.

Research shows that women block other women in leadership when the organisation has a lack of female senior position seats and is competitive (Kramer and Harris 2019).

Inclusive leaders acknowledge their journey and what it took for them to get to where they are right now. I call them "obstacle removers". They also hold themselves accountable for sharing their learnings from this journey with others and removing their career challenges beforehand.

Working in multinational companies as a manager adds another responsibility for inclusive leaders, which is mediation in conflict situations.

Let me share another story with you. One day, I was in a stand-up team meeting where everyone had to share what tasks they had done the previous day and what tasks they were going to work on that day. When it came to this person's turn, she accused me of not completing a task on time and called me "lazy" in front of all the team members.

After a brief moment of shock, I looked into the eyes of my manager to see if he had anything to say to correct this toxic behaviour. He acted as usual and did not even have a word with either of us afterwards. He did not hold himself accountable for mediating this situation. As a result, he lost my trust as well as that of other team members.

Things happen. We make mistakes. However, in inclusive workplaces, there is no tolerance for personal accusations and finger pointing. That's where the importance of accountable inclusive leaders comes in. They do hold themselves accountable in situations like the one in this story.

Here are some ideas to improve your team's and your accountability in diversity and inclusion.

Action: Make it clear

Make sure your team is clear on the organisation's diversity and inclusion vision, goals and their roles to make it happen.

Reflection: Ask your team the following questions:

- How do they feel about the organisation's diversity and inclusion vision? Does it align with them?
- What does inclusion look like in their daily tasks?
- How do they think they are doing currently? Why?
- What are their blockers?
- Can they recognise an inclusive role model within the organisation? What are they doing differently?

Action: Recognise and reward

Recognising and rewarding inclusive behaviours is also an indication of accountability.

Tips and tools: An idea for building an environment for your team that appreciates inclusive behaviours could be to add a dedicated section to your Friday afternoon 'thank you' team feedback reminder (mentioned in a previous example) to praise inclusive behaviour on the part of another team member.

Reflection: Reflect on how you can put this into practice.

How do you currently reward and recognise your team members' work?

What will you do differently?

Summary

An inclusive leader is someone who does not wait for others to ask them to take action towards the diversity and inclusion vision of their organisation. They hold themselves accountable first and are a good role model for their team. They also inspire and motivate others to understand inclusion at a deeper level and take action. They recognise inclusive behaviours and build an environment that rewards these behaviours.

Activity: Accountability self-assessment

Inclusive leaders hold themselves accountable for their contribution to the organisation's diversity and inclusion vision and strategy.

Asking your team the following questions can help you understand where you are in terms of your accountability:

- What does diversity and inclusion mean for me? Why?
- Do I know the diversity and inclusion vision of my company?
- Do I feel this vision aligns with my values?
- How can I embed these values into my daily tasks?
- Am I aware of the activities around the topic? What are the activities?
- Is my team setting goals or taking actions towards the company's diversity and inclusion goals?
- How is my team doing compared to other teams? Why?
- How can I make sure that my team is embedding diversity and inclusion goals in their daily tasks?
- Do I track my progress and the team's progress on this?
- Who is my inclusive leader role model?
- Who is my go-to person who can help me and my team?
- Does my team know where they can find learning materials and get help on this?
- Am I the go-to person for my team to get help? Why? Why not?

Note for your journal: Write your answers down in a journal and look at them regularly to remind yourself.

Interview with Adaku Ezeudo, CEO at PhoenixRize, Diversity, Equity and Inclusion Consulting

Furkan Karayel: What does accountability mean for an inclusive leader?

Adaku Ezeudo: Inclusive leadership is a critical capability helping companies and organisations adapt to diverse talents, ideas, customers and markets and improve diversity and inclusion (D&I) goals. However, for D&I goals to be realised, leadership must first hold themselves accountable for achieving those goals and cascading D&I expectations throughout the organisation. By taking accountability for goals, an inclusive leader signals the importance of D&I as a business priority.

Accountability for an inclusive leader begins with introspection and self-reflection of thoughts, emotions, behaviours and actions and how they impact their peers, employees and organisational culture.

They are willing to ask themselves tough questions and lean into the discomfort of engaging in uncomfortable conversations knowing that it is in the discomfort that the learning and the growing happens. They recognise the different working styles and skills of their employees and ensure that everyone is treated with fairness and respect. They foster an atmosphere where all employees can work at peak productivity without being distracted by microaggressions or discrimination.

Accountability for an inclusive leader goes beyond the individual actions and decisions of leaders. An inclusive leader holds employees accountable for their behaviour, development and work processes. They ensure all employees understand what unacceptable behaviour is, they communicate the business, ethical and legal case for diversity and challenge employees who do not demonstrate commitment to D&I. They promote psychological safety in the workplace and encourage employees to adapt to the needs of others and work collaboratively through challenges.

FK: What should leaders do to gain more accountability for diversity and inclusion?

AE: Act as a role model for diversity and inclusion:

Organisational culture begins and ends with leadership. Leaders must display the behaviours they wish to see in others. Leaders should speak, act and operate in an authentic, respectful and ethical manner, be accepting of others' differences and uniqueness and be adaptable, agile and flexible enough to embrace change.

Develop and nurture inclusive workplace policies and practices:

Leaders should also be willing to design, develop and implement strategies, systems, and sustainable policies, processes, and practices that nurture diversity, inclusion, equality and, full and fair opportunity for their employees, customers and stakeholders. They should also prepare to mitigate opportunities for bias, exclusion, discrimination and harassment in the workplace, and cultivate an environment of psychological safety where every employee can thrive.

Empower inclusive future leaders:

To create companies and organisations where everyone can achieve their potential, it is critical that those with aspirations to lead understand how to create an inclusive work environment. Through tailored inclusive leadership programmes for future leaders, they can learn how to deliver on D&I commitments, set and communicate expectations, and hold their direct reports accountable for the results they commit to.

What is your takeaway from this chapter?

If you reflect and share your learnings regularly, they stay in your memory longer and you start internalising them.

Reflect and share your learning experience below.

INCLUSIVE LEADERS TURN
DOUBTERS INTO BELIEVERS.

CHAPTER SIX: **COMMITMENT**

Introduction

Can you think of a person who is committed to diversity and inclusion in your organisation?

What do they do differently from others?

In this final chapter of the Inclusive Intelligence book, we will talk about commitment, why is it important for your Inclusive Intelligence, how you can develop a vision and your commitment to making a difference in diversity and inclusion.

Let's do it.

"There is a difference between interest and commitment. When you are interested in doing something, you do it only when it is convenient. When you are committed to something, you accept no excuses; only results."

Kenneth Blanchard

If I say "Greta Thunberg", what is the next word that appears in your mind? What about "Elon Musk"?

You can see how their vision became part of their identity, as we cannot think of them without thinking of their vision.

Commitment means emotionally connecting to a vision that we want to see happening and being willing to change our own behaviours to create change.

A simple example. I am connected with many executives of big organisations on LinkedIn and I see that some of them regularly share great insights, ideas and their learnings on diversity and inclusion. These are not heartless copy-paste posts, though. You can easily see that diversity and inclusion is in their daily agenda and they are committed to it.

Vision is to a leader like water to a fish. We cannot think of a leader without a vision. In fact, vision makes leaders. So far, we talked about self-awareness, empathy, cultural wisdom and accountability as characteristics of a leader. All of them have a relatively low visibility to another person. Whereas commitment is the most visible skill of all. That is why a leader's commitment to diversity and inclusion has a greater impact, as it is contagious at all levels of the organisation.

Inclusive leaders are the ones who have a diversity and inclusion vision, the courage to talk about it publicly and who take their talk forward by showing their commitment and treating diversity and inclusion goals as a business case.

According to Russell Reynolds Associates' World's Most Admired Companies Inclusion Index, successful companies are the ones that show real commitment to diversity and inclusion. In the same research the participants rated the current status of leadership commitment, voice and influence and organisational fairness practices as relatively low compared to workplace respect, working across differences and employee recruitment, development and retention (Polonskaia and Royal 2019).

In other research about leadership commitment, the participants said they feel their leaders are simply paying lip service to diversity and inclusion but are not personally invested in advancing it (ALLY Council 2018). Commitment to diversity was also associated with having more women leaders in large public companies in the research conducted from 2015 to 2017.

Ali is a senior financial consultant at a big firm. He says that diversity and inclusion are close to his heart because he experienced being the only representative of his identity in his previous job. He has only been working in his new role for three months.

Unfortunately, Ali's new manager does not believe diversity and inclusion could bring any value to his team. Ali finds himself working long hours to meet his manager's expectations while trying his best to bring diversity and inclusion to the team.

His diligent work in the area is not recognised by his manager and his peers. In fact, his peers told Ali that, "It is not going to work with this manager. This will not have any impact on your promotion, so your efforts are useless."

What if Ali's manager was more open to conversations about diversity and inclusion? You can see the impact of a manager here.

Here are some ideas of what you could do to show your commitment to a diversity and inclusion vision:

Action: Set up a vision for you and your team

Bring your team together in a meeting to co-create a vision. This offers a unique experience of brainstorming together to understand their approaches and commitment to the topic.

Tips and tools: When the vision statement comes from the team, they own it. They are more likely to internalise it and feel part of the success towards the vision strategy.

My favourite vision statement is by Johnson & Johnson (Johnson & Johnson 2021): "Be yourself, change the world."

You can find more examples of the best vision statements in the References and Further Reading section.

Another example is CEO Action. It is an organisation that brings CEOs of the biggest companies to sign a pledge of commitment to taking actions in diversity and inclusion (CEO Action for Diversity and Inclusion 2020).

Reflection: Write down your diversity and inclusion vision for you and your team.

Action: Courage and voice

To encourage your team as a leader, first you must open up a conversation about your own story and your commitment. People absolutely love and remember personal stories.

Tips and tools: Seeing the CEO of an organisation or a C-Suite level executive being vocal about diversity and inclusion more often in the agenda, joining/leading internal/external events and repeating the vision regularly with employees sets a great example.

Remember, this is a journey and you cannot achieve this alone.

Reflection: Share the story of your commitment to diversity and inclusion with your team. This will motivate others to open up in the team/organisation to do so as well. What have you learned in the process?

Action: Reward commitment

As an inclusive leader, recognising and rewarding team commitment to diversity and inclusion is crucial for empowering and encouraging more employees to prioritise this on the agenda and change their behaviours.

Tips and tools: It can be in the form of weekly thank you emails, gift vouchers, as well as perhaps sponsoring a conference trip where they can speak about their experiences of cultivating an inclusive environment.

Ask your team about how they would like to be rewarded. You will be really surprised to hear what they have to say.

Summary

Inclusive leaders' commitment is an emotional connection to their diversity and inclusion vision. Setting up concrete goals for the year, sharing their diversity and inclusion stories often and rewarding the team's progress are some of the actions inclusive leaders can take to show their commitment and inspire others in the organisation.

Activity: Inclusive leaders goal setting activity

"What gets measured gets done."

Without planning actions and goals in a calendar, the goals and vision can easily be missed.

Inclusive leaders allow employees to have their own space to set and track their progress and help them remove obstacles from their path.

Tips and tools: We designed a worksheet for you to set your goals and milestones. It allows you to break down each goal into small actions on a weekly basis and keep track of all your achievements.

At the end of our workshops, we always ask our participants to share one action they will commit to from today. These examples can help you set your milestones and goals too. Visit the Diversein YouTube channel for examples (Diversein 2019).

Inclusive Leader's Journal

Inclusiveintelligence.org

- Set **SMART** goals: **S**pecific, **M**easurable, **A**chievable, **R**elevant,**T**ime-based
- Set a milestone at the end of each month
- Take an action every week towards the goal

Goal 1		Month 1	Month 2	Month 3
	Week 1			
	Week 2			
	Week 3			
	Week 4			

Goal 2		Month 1	Month 2	Month 3
	Week 1			
	Week 2			
	Week 3			
	Week 4			

Goal 3		Month 1	Month 2	Month 3
	Week 1			
	Week 2			
	Week 3			
	Week 4			

Goal 4		Month 1	Month 2	Month 3
	Week 1			
	Week 2			
	Week 3			
	Week 4			

Interview with Adrian Whelan, senior vice president, Brown Brothers Harriman

Furkan Karayel: Adrian, what is the impact of a leader's commitment to diversity and inclusion?

Adrian Whelan: A leader's commitment to inclusion normally results in better results. In the corporate business world that I live in, and I am big into sports, what you can see when a leader truly commits to diversity and inclusion? It results in better outcomes, so that is one thing.

The other thing is that any tone from the top needs to be consistent, and without tone from the top change simply does not happen, change of any kind. So, to really drive inclusion and diversity, you do need that tone from the top, and it has to be consistent and sincere.

The last point I'd make is the trickle-down effect. If leaders truly believe and are consistent in their messaging and are vocal and public about inclusion, diversity and about change, then it empowers people throughout the organisation to have the moral courage to advocate for that change. It's often referred to as psychological safety, and when leaders and top-down encourage that kind of inclusive behaviour the trickle-down effect can be enormous.

FK: I have seen you speaking at many different events, I see how you are committed to diversity and inclusion. How did you achieve this? How can other leaders gain a diverse and inclusive vision and show their commitment to it?

AW: It's interesting you say that I am a fairly or very vocal advocate of inclusion. I was not always. I come from an underrepresented or marginalised community myself. I come from Finglas and work in financial services. There are not a lot of people from where I was born in my industry.

I made a decision at one point in time to not be quiet and shy and ashamed of my background, and actually it empowered me once I found the moral courage to speak up.

It gave me great wellbeing to do this. It made me feel better personally, then I saw the impact that it could have by being an ally and a mentor and even an ambassador or a role model, any of those words for other people in my community.

The other thing that I found is that it grows your own social network professionally or just in life. You start meeting people who have similar shared values as yourself. That can be helpful and usually empowering.

You can also have commercial networks and it can actually be beneficial. If I'm honest, in my own career it's benefited me as well. That is quite selfish, but again it has.

And again, the sense of helping somebody else is hugely powerful. If you are a leader, you do get paid back for the work you do, you can see discernible change either at an individual level or in an organisation that you are working on.

The other thing that drives me is interesting, as Liverpool picked up the trophy there the other day. Jürgen Klopp is an inspirational and inclusive leader and when he took on that Liverpool job at the time, he said that what he really wanted to do is make doubters into believers.

What he said for Liverpool's fans, players, everyone in their organisation, was that they doubted whether they could do what they have just done this week (2020). He has been an inclusive and vocal supporter of being your authentic self, of working as a group, and he is the leader. He works with people and empowers people.

And again, turning doubters into believers is something that a vocal champion of inclusion needs to do because there are many people, let's be honest, who continue to doubt that this diversity inclusion results in better outcomes, but those that do believe see it in their lives, in their organisations every day, and that's why I remain a vocal advocate.

What is your takeaway from this chapter?

If you reflect and share your learnings regularly, they stay in your memory longer and you start internalising them.

Reflect and share your learning experience below.

Conclusion

Remember Inclusive Intelligence is a journey and you took your first step by reading this book. Congratulations!

What's next now?

One commitment: What is your one takeaway from this book? The one thing you will commit to today?

Share your achievement: Share your takeaway from this book on LinkedIn, Twitter, Instagram or other social media channels with the #InclusiveIntelligence hashtag. Feel free to tag us too.

Share your feedback: We welcome your feedback to deliver our best for you. Email: diversein.com@gmail.com

Consider taking the Inclusive Intelligence Online Course: Take the Inclusive Intelligence online course at inclusiveintelligence.org

Connect with us:

http://diversein.com

https://www.linkedin.com/company/diversein-com/

http://furkankarayel.com

http://linkedin.com/in/karayelfurkan/

http://twitter.com/furkankarayel

Invite us to your organisation: We provide workshops and talks to small/large groups to help you discover the potentials of diverse teams and help them practise their Inclusive Intelligence interactively. Say hello at: diversein.com@gmail.com

I look forward to meeting you in person.

Warmest regards,

Furkan Karayel

Keywords

Introduction: What is Inclusive Intelligence?

Inclusive Intelligence, diversity, inclusion, inclusive leadership, talent retention, job satisfaction, psychological safety, belonging, authenticity, leadership

Chapter one: Self-Awareness

Self-awareness, core values, bias, Johari Window, blind spots, motivators, strengths, weaknesses, Myers-Briggs test, feedback, Harvard Business School Implicit Association test, reflection, authenticity, Don Quixote, fitting in, status quo, organisational culture, acceptance, emotional labour, leadership, authentic self, true self

Chapter two: Empathy

Empathy, Emotional Intelligence, self-empathy, empathy in leadership, naturally empathetics, underestimaters, adaptable, reading emotions, bias, multicultural environment, cultural wisdom, job interview, allyship, taste-base inclusion, mentorship

Chapter three: Engagement

Engagement, collaboration, employee engagement, engagement in human level, open, closed up, employee performance meeting, instant feedback, small talk, interaction, recognition, online tools, feedback, mentorship

Chapter four: Cultural Wisdom

Cultural wisdom, cultural intelligence, culture, background, emotional labour, harmony, belonging, cultural differences, communication channels, stereotypes, unconscious bias, bias, microaggression, culture map

Chapter five: Accountability

Accountability, responsibility, lip service, inclusive mindset, employee resource group, obstacle removers, mediation, conflict, vision, alignment, role model, reward

Chapter six: Commitment

Commitment, vision, leadership, leaders, diversity and inclusion goals, business case, lip service, pledge of commitment, action, courage, personal story, measurement, journal

References and Further Reading

We have compiled all the references mentioned in this book and a very rich list of further reading materials and tools to give you easy access online. Please visit: https://www.diversein.com/bookreferences

References

Introduction: What is Inclusive Intelligence?

Bourke, Juliet. 2018. 'The Diversity and Inclusion Revolution: Eight Powerful Truths.' *Deloitte Review*. January 22, 2018. https://www2.deloitte.com/us/en/insights/deloitte-review/issue-22/diversity-and-inclusion-at-work-eight-powerful-truths.html.

Boushey, Heather, and Sarah Jane Glynn. 2012. *There are Significant Business Costs to Replacing Employees*. Washington, DC: Center for American Progress. https://www.americanprogress.org/wp-content/uploads/2012/11/CostofTurnover.pdf.

Cruz, Esther L., Allison Schnidman, Akansha Agrawal, and Bo De Koning. 2015. *Why & How People Change*. New York, NY: LinkedIn Talent Solutions. https://business.linkedin.com/content/dam/business/talent-solutions/global/en_us/job-switchers/PDF/job-switchers-global-report-English.pdf.

Dixon-Fyle, Sundiatu, Kevin Dolan, Vivian Hunt, and Sara Prince. 2020. *Diversity Wins: How Inclusion Matters*. New York, NY: McKinsey & Company. https://www.mckinsey.com/featured-insights/diversity-and-inclusion/diversity-wins-how-inclusion-matters.

Gaudiano, Paolo. 2020. 'How Inclusion Improves Diversity and Company Performance.' *Forbes*. July 13, 2020. https://www.

forbes.com/sites/paologaudiano/2020/07/13/how-inclusion-improves-diversity-and-company-performance/

Jonsen, Karsten, Martha Maznevski, Günter K. Stahl, and Andreas Voigt. 2007. *Unravelling the Diversity-Performance Link in Multicultural Teams: Meta-Analysis of Studies on the Impact of Cultural Diversity in Teams.* Fontainebleau, France: INSEAD. https://www.worldcat.org/title/unraveling-the-diversity-performance-link-in-multicultural-teams-meta-analysis-of-studies-on-the-impact-of-cultural-diversity-in-teams/oclc/837490342.

Menzies, Felicity. 2018. 'How Does Employee Well-Being Link to Diversity and Inclusion?' *Include-Empower* (blog), Culture Plus Consulting. August 17, 2018. https://cultureplusconsulting.com/2018/08/17/how-does-employee-wellbeing-link-to-diversity-and-inclusion/.

Peterson, Becky. 2017. "Travis Kalanick Lasted in his Role for 6.5 Years – Five Times Longer Than the Average Uber Employee." *Business Insider.* August 20, 2017. https://www.businessinsider.com/employee-retention-rate-top-tech-companies-2017-8.

Chapter one: Self-Awareness

George, Bill. 2015. *Discover Your True North.* San Francisco, CA: Jossey-Bass.

Project Implicit. 2011. 'Implicit Association Test.' Accessed July 5, 2021. https://implicit.harvard.edu/implicit/selectatest.html.

Truity. 2020. 'The TypeFinder® Personality Test: Beyond Briggs Myers' 16 Types, Find Your True Strengths.' Accessed July 5, 2021. https://www.truity.com/test/type-finder-personality-test-new.

Wikimedia Foundation. 2021. 'Johari Window.' Wikipedia. Last modified July 4, 2021. https://en.wikipedia.org/wiki/Johari_window.

Zenger, Jack, and Joe Folkman. 2019. *The 11 Components of a Best-in Class 360-Degree Assessment.* Orem, UT: Zenger Folkman. https://zengerfolkman.com/wp-content/uploads/2019/08/The-11-Components_WP-2019.pdf.

Chapter two: Empathy

Brown, Brené. 2015. *Daring Greatly: How the Courage to Be Vulnerable Transforms the Way We Live, Love, Parent, and Lead.* New York, NY: Avery.

Goleman, Daniel. 2005. *Emotional Intelligence: Why It Can Matter More Than IQ.* New York, NY: Random House Publishing Group.

Keltner, Dacher. 2016. *The Power Paradox: How We Gain and Lose Influence.* London: Penguin Books.

Pounds, Jerry. 2014. *'Empathy: skill or personality trait?'.* Accessed July 9, 2021. https://www.management-issues.com/opinion/3237/empathy-skill-or-personality-trait/

Leading Effectively Staff. 2020. 'Why Empathy in the Workplace Matters.' *Center for Creative Leadership.* www.ccl.org/articles/leading-effectively-articles/empathy-in-the-workplace-a-tool-for-effective-leadership/.

Sinar, Evan, Rich Wellins, Matthew Paese, Audrey Smith, and Bruce Watt. 2016. *High-Resolution Leadership: A Synthesis of 15,000 Assessments into How Leaders Shape the Business Landscape.* Bridgeville, PA: Development Dimensions International. https://media.ddiworld.com/research/high-resolution-leadership-2015-2016_tr_ddi.pdf.

Chapter three: Engagement

Gallup. 2017. 'What Is Employee Engagement and How Do You Improve It?' Accessed July 5, 2021. www.gallup.com/workplace/285674/improve-employee-engagement-workplace.aspx

Heinz, Kate. 2021. 'Best Employee Engagement Tools to Implement in 2021.' *Built In*. Last updated June 2, 2021. https://builtin.com/employee-engagement/employee-engagement-tools.

Peterson, Becky. 2017. 'Travis Kalanick Lasted in his Role for 6.5 Years – Five Times Longer Than the Average Uber Employee.' *Business Insider*. August 20, 2017. https://www.businessinsider.com/employee-retention-rate-top-tech-companies-2017-8.

Seppälä, Emma. 2014. 'What Bosses Gain by Being Vulnerable.' *Harvard Business Review*. December 11, 2014. https://hbr.org/2014/12/what-bosses-gain-by-being-vulnerable.

Chapter four: Cultural Wisdom

Diversein. 2021. 'What Does Racial Microaggression Look Like?' Accessed July 5, 2021. https://www.diversein.com/post/what-does-racial-microaggression-look-like.

Livermore, David. 2009. *Leading with Cultural Intelligence: The New Secret to Success*. New York, NY: AMACOM Books.

Merriam-Webster. n.d. 'Microaggression (noun).' Accessed July 5, 2021. https://www.merriam-webster.com/dictionary/microaggression.

Meyer, Erin. 2016. *Culture Map: Decoding How People Think, Lead, and Get Things Done Across Cultures*. New York, NY: PublicAffairs.

Chapter five: Accountability

Dive, Brian. 2008. *The Accountable Leader: Developing Effective Leadership Through Managerial Accountability*. London: Kogan Page Publishers.

Kramer, Andrea S., and Alton B. Harris. 2019. *It's Not You It's the Workplace: Women's Conflict at Work and the Bias That Built It*. London: Nicholas Brealey. https://www.managementtoday.co.uk/why-women-sabotage-workplace/women-in-business/article/1669093

Molinaro, Vince. 2017. The Leadership Accountability Gap: A Global Study Exploring the Real State of Leadership in Organizations Today. Maitland, FL: Lee Hecht Harrison. https://www.lhh.com/lhhpenna/en/-/media/lhh/uk/pdfs/lhh-leadership-accountability-global-research-report.pdf.

Chapter six: Commitment

ALLY Council. 2018. 'Diversity in the Workplace: Without Accountability, It's Just Lip Service.' https://allyenergy.com/diversity-in-the-workplace-without-accountability-its-just-lip-service/.

CEO: Action for Diversity and Inclusion. 2020. "Homepage." Accessed July 5, 2021. https://www.ceoaction.com.

Johnson & Johnson. 2021. *Diversity, Equity & Inclusion Policy*. New Brunswick, NJ: Johnson & Johnson. https://www.jnj.com/about-jnj/policies-and-positions/diversity-equity-and-inclusion-policy

Polonskaia, Alina, and Mark Royal. 2019. 'How the World's Most Admired Companies Drive D&I.' *Human Resources Executive*. December 10, 2019. https://hrexecutive.com/how-the-worlds-most-admired-companies-drive-diversity-and-inclusion/.

Diversein. 2019. 'Diversity and Inclusion for Sales Managers. One goal you can commit today.' YouTube, December 3, 2019. https://www.youtube.com/watch?v=fh5ZF7Lb97w.

About the Author

Furkan Karayel is a multi-award-winning inclusive leadership advisor and CEO at Diversein.com and the author of the book *Inclusive Intelligence: How to Be a Role Model for Diversity and Inclusion in the Workplace*. Furkan lectures for the Equality, Diversity and Inclusion Master's programme at Dún Laoghaire Institute of Art, Design + Technology. Her passions are leveraging women in leadership, diversity and empowering female founders globally.

Furkan founded Diversein.com after 10 years of software engineering experience in multinational tech companies in Ireland. She has been honoured with "Diversity and Inclusion Role Model in Business", "Speaker of the Year" and "Trailblazer in Women in Tech" Awards.

Additionally, Furkan is an active keynote speaker at global conferences and corporate events where she shares her learnings and insights about experiences of the tech world as a woman, her recommendations for Inclusive Intelligence and leadership, and the power of diversity and inclusion in the workplace.

Personal website: furkankarayel.com

LinkedIn: linkedin.com/in/karayelfurkan/

Twitter: twitter.com/furkankarayel/

Business website: diversein.com